THE THREE SAVIOURS ARE HERE!

BY
HIS EMINENCE, SIR GEORGE KING, Ph.D.

PRINTED AND PUBLISHED BY
THE AETHERIUS SOCIETY
757 Fulham Road, London S.W.6, England.
Telephone: 01-736 4187/01-731 1094.

First Published in 1967
Revised Edition April 1982

COPYRIGHT OWNED BY
HIS EMINENCE, SIR GEORGE KING, Ph.D.
METROPOLITAN ARCHBISHOP OF THE AETHERIUS CHURCHES

Copyright ©1967 and ©1982 by His Eminence, Sir George King.

All rights strictly reserved. No reproduction or translation in any form, be it in whole or in part, is allowed without first obtaining the written permission from the author, His Eminence, Sir George King.
"THE THREE SAVIOURS ARE HERE!" is printed and published by The Aetherius Society, 6202 Afton Place, Hollywood, California 90028. U.S.A.

Manufactured in the United States of America

THE THREE SAVIOURS

ARE HERE!

Written by
His Eminence, Sir George King, Ph.D.

By the same Author:
THE DAY THE GODS CAME
THE NINE FREEDOMS
YOU ARE RESPONSIBLE!
THE FIVE TEMPLES OF GOD
YOU TOO CAN HEAL
THE TWELVE BLESSINGS
WISDOM OF THE PLANETS
LIFE ON THE PLANETS
OPERATION SUNBEAM—GOD'S MAGIC IN ACTION
FLYING SAUCERS
THE PRACTICES OF AETHERIUS
SPACE CONTACT IN SANTA BARBARA
CONTACT YOUR HIGHER SELF THROUGH YOGA
THE AGE OF AETHERIUS
BECOME A BUILDER OF THE NEW AGE
THIS IS THE HOUR OF TRUTH
BOOK OF SACRED PRAYERS
COSMIC VOICE, VOLUME 1
COSMIC VOICE, VOLUME 2
A SPECIAL ASSIGNMENT
MY CONTACT WITH THE GREAT WHITE BROTHERHOOD
A SERIES OF LESSONS ON SPIRITUAL SCIENCE—ON CASSETTES

All books and cassettes by His Eminence, Sir George King, Ph.D. are obtainable from the publishers, The Aetherius Society:
American Headquarters: 6202 Afton Place, Hollywood, California 90028. U.S.A.
European Headquarters: 757 Fulham Road, London SW6 5UU, England.

CONTENTS

Chapter		Page
	INTRODUCTION	7-11
	FOREWORD	12-14
1.	ANOTHER BLESSING BY THE MASTER JESUS	15-21
2.	THE TRUTHS OF SAINT GOO-LING	22-35
3.	THE TRUTHS OF JESUS	36-79
4.	OPERATION KARMALIGHT	80-85
5.	FURTHER ACTION BY THE SIX ADEPTS	86-96

This book is reverently dedicated to the Master Jesus and Saint Goo-Ling Who in deep compassion for humanity gave the far-reaching revelations herein to enable man to help in the preparation of a Glorious Future

INTRODUCTION TO THE AUTHOR

The author of this book was born in Wellington, Shropshire, England, on January 23rd, 1919. From an early age he displayed a deep interest in Religion, at first of an orthodox nature. Later, when he had studied deeply what are today known as the metaphysical sciences, he turned to a close study and diligent practise of certain forms of Yoga. For many hours each day, over a period of many years, this mystical science was the evolutionary ladder up which he climbed in order to learn about the higher aspects of the many and varied forms of life which abound upon and around this Planet. This deep interest seemed as natural to him as another might study chemistry or engineering. But, without his realization at the time, he was in actuality preparing to take upon himself an amazing destiny which was to re-shape the whole of his life into an unwavering intensity of purpose and dedication aimed at bringing about a Spiritual Renaissance upon Earth.

In 1954 the time was ripe and the student was ready. He experienced the first recognizable mental contact with Cosmic Intelligences Who live in other parts of the Solar System. He was declared by these mighty Beings of Ancient Wisdom to be "Primary Terrestrial Mental Channel" — the Voice of Interplanetary Parliament through which They would direct Their message to the people of Earth.

The story of this contact has been told and re-told by the media, hundreds of times in many different languages, and has been repeated hundreds of times by lecturers on the public platforms throughout the United States, Great Britain, Nigeria, New Zealand, Australia, Holland and other European countries. There is no need to repeat it here, save to say that the Watchers, or Rishis, of the Ancient Texts — the Heavenly Hosts of the Christian Bible — had appointed a new channel of communication to mankind in the hour of desperate need!

From that initial contact the author, already capable of consciously bringing about the deep meditative state of Samadhi, was used as a mental channel for over 600 Transmissions given by Intelligences residing on worlds more highly evolved than this Earth. Some of these Transmissions have been published, both in printed texts as well as on audio cassettes which have circulated throughout many countries and have brought hope, positive Spiritual direction and enlightenment to thousands of people.

In 1955, The Aetherius Society was founded by the author in England and later incorporated in 1960 in the United States. Since that time, The Aetherius Society has been responsible for the preservation and publication of these great Cosmic Transmissions, all of which are Teachings of profundity, yet given in such a way that they can be understood and acted upon by any thinking researcher.

As well as being made responsible for receiving Cosmic Transmissions, the author was also given many other assignments by Cosmic Intelligences, all fully described in literature published by The Aetherius Society.

Early in 1966, the author invented and designed a Mission which was to become world renowned for its importance. This Mission was officially named "Operation Sunbeam" and accepted by Higher Forces into the overall Cosmic Plan for the advancement, enlightenment and salvation of mankind. Although described in detail elsewhere, in brief, "Operation Sunbeam" is a Mission in which Spiritual Energies, of the highest frequencies, are collected and given, through certain known Psychic Centres of the living Planet, to The Logos Of Earth as a token repayment for what this mighty Cosmic Being has done for all life upon this Planet. "Operation Sunbeam" has been described by Higher Forces as being the most important task being performed upon the Earth today; more important than anything being done by any government or any country!

It is little wonder then, that the author was instructed to hold himself in readiness for an invitation to an assembly arranged by the Highest Powers on this Earth in order to extend the range, potency and possibilities of the Mission, "Operation Sunbeam," which the author had designed.

The call came on December 5th, 1978. The author projected his consciousness from his physical body to that mystical floating Temple called "Shamballa" which, for thousands of years, has been the headquarters through which The Spiritual Hierarchy of this Earth operates. There, the author was received with love and understanding by the Members of The Great White Brotherhood, as the Ascended Masters of

Earth are often known and referred to.

The main reason for the invitation was to ask the author, the designer of "Operation Sunbeam," if They, The Spiritual Hierarchy Of Earth, may have his permission to advance "Operation Sunbeam" in such a way which would not be possible for The Aetherius Society with its limited funding and resources. After all necessary occult protocols had been strictly observed and the author's permission had been given, he was — to his utter amazement — approached by the Kumara of Shamballa Who physically touched him three times; once upon the head, then upon the right shoulder and then upon the left shoulder, and spoke in a physical voice in perfect English, these most significant words:

"I thus Initiate you as Grand Knight Templar Of The Inner Sanctum Of The Holy Order Of The Spiritual Hierarchy Of Earth."

This mystical Knighthood was bestowed upon the author for his devotion to and cooperation with The Cosmic Masters since 1954 and especially for his work in "Operation Sunbeam" which had helped to bring about a stabilization of conditions upon the Planet Earth.

As above, so below!

What occurs on the inner planes is also later manifested on the mento-physical realms.

In incredibly quick succession, the author was given a Knighthood in 12 established Orders of Chivalry, usually at a rank equivalent to or above that of "Knight Commander." Certain of these Orders of Chivalry gave him the elevated title of "Knight Commander, Grand Cross of Justice." He received the legitimate noble title of, and was officially Crowned, "Count de Florina" by one of the world's noble Princes. Many coveted civil awards, such as the French L'Etoile de la Paix," were given him, as well as the prestigious "Prize of Peace and Justice" which, in the past, had been received by Doctor Albert Schweitzer, Professor Albert Einstein, Doctor Henry Kissinger and Mother Theresa of Calcutta.

The author was consecrated and created as an Archbishop and released to found his own Religion, whereafter he became Metropolitan Archbishop of The Aetherius Churches worldwide. Distinguished decorations, such as the Order of "Polonia Restituta" from the Government of the Republic of Poland (in exile), were given him and he was elected "Minister of the Year for 1981" by a worldwide religious denomination of Ministers from 49 countries.

On Saturday, September 26th, 1981, the Coronation of the author as "His Serene Highness Prince George King de Santorini" was performed by His Royal and Imperial Highness Prince Henri III Paleologue at St. George's Church, Hanover Square, London. Shortly thereafter the author founded his own Order of Chivalry, "The Mystical Order of Saint Peter," which received an extension from His Royal and Imperial Highness Prince Henri III Paleologue of the "Fons Honorum" (Fountain of Honours), thereby making this Order of Chivalry high among the most legitimate Orders on Earth today.

Thus, in only two years after the initial Ceremony of Knighthood held on Shamballa, His Serene Highness Prince Doctor George King de Santorini was given the highest honours which are possible to give to any man who was not born into nobility.

Indeed there was a Master Plan at work which inspired people in position to recognize the devotion of an individual and to come forward most boldly with this recognition.

These are some of the many high honours which were bestowed upon the Founder-President of The Aetherius Society by great people who had come to recognize him for what he was — a man completely dedicated to God and to the salvation of humanity.

Years before this, he had been recognized, carefully analyzed and later chosen by Cosmic Forces as, "Primary Terrestrial Mental Channel" and it is in the capacity of "Primary Terrestrial Mental Channel" that he writes this book, "The Three Saviours Are Here!"

This book, when first published in 1967, did not contain an introduction to the author. Now, in the 1982 edition of the book, with the author's status so much changed, both in the eyes of the world as well as on the Higher Planes of Earth and beyond, it is felt that this introduction is important for a fuller appreciation of its contents.

A large part of the events forecast in this book have come to pass.

The Three Saviours fought Their battle and won.

Each separate action against the forces of evil was reported in detail through "Primary Terrestrial Mental Channel" and recorded for posterity — for a future time when these Transmissions of the Armageddon will be studied and revered by a more enlightened human race.

The Three Adepts Themselves, "The Three Saviours" of this volume, are now Six Adepts in number, all of Whom continue Their unceasing watchfulness and protection of humanity, not only against the forces of darkness and evil, still active and powerful upon Earth, but also against dangers to mankind from other sources as well. In addition, They have come to work very closely with the author and The Aetherius Society in some major World Missions where Their expertise and vast Wisdom has helped greatly to assist mankind slowly forward in the direction of the coming Golden Millennium of World Peace and Enlightenment. Nearly all Their actions, in amazing detail and with profound understanding, have been recorded in one way or another for posterity by the author, who has come to know Them intimately, and who has won Their deepest respect.

Such is the man who has written this book. Read on in reverence to the great Cosmic Plan which has made this edition possible.

Had The Three Saviours failed, you would not now be reading this — or any other Holy Work for that matter!

FOREWORD

The two Transmissions, explained in detail in this book, delivered by Saint Goo-Ling and the Master Jesus, through George King, the President of The Aetherius Society, on September 23rd, 1967, constitute two of the most vital Transmissions of Cosmic wisdom ever given to this Planet in the history of terrestrial man. Any thinking man, studying these Transmissions, must admit that the implications given herein are greater than most hitherto from any source.

Some of you may wonder why a relatively small organization, like The Aetherius Society, was entrusted with messages of such obvious importance to humanity as these. The only answer to this question can be a logical one. Man has no right to question the wisdom of Masters such as Saint Goo-Ling or the Master Jesus. As a matter of fact, it is the fallibility in the thinking processes of mankind which has brought on the conditions referred to by both of these great Beings.

For two thousand years man has questioned the words of Jesus. Some have even tried to prove His non-existence. Very few have adopted His Commandments in thought, word and deed. If the majority had done so, then the world would be a much better place than it is today and the clash between good and evil described herein, shortly due to come about, would not need to take place. If a Cosmic Master, of the proven ability of Jesus, sees fit to release such truths as those given here through a relatively small organization, instead of through the United Nations, for instance, then we should realize that the Master made this move because He saw that it was the best way to bring about the results which He deemed necessary. Instead of questioning the words herein, if we spent the next few months of our lives living in the light of the wisdom given, we would, at the end of that time, no longer question these words as they would have been proven truthful in every way to every man.

If countries, instead of questioning the birth and existence of Jesus throughout the centuries, had lived by His teachings—His very existence would have been proven to all men in all ways; would have been proven to the world, so definitely, that there would not be a man on Earth who would not believe in His existence today. So excellent would be the conditions prevailing on the surface of this Earth, that no sane person would question the Master's wisdom.

It is the same thing, exactly, with these two Transmissions. Both these Masters wanted to bring about a result which They, in Their great wisdom, could foresee as the best result to be brought about. Therefore, They chose to release this information through The Aetherius Society.

Up to the time of writing this book, no directive has been given to us, by either of these Masters, to spread this word through local news media, such as television. Not that this word is secret, if it were, it would not have been given in the way it was given. This is obvious logic. But it seems that it was given through The Aetherius Society because the Masters saw fit to use the Society in this way, because the Masters could trust that this word would be given out as They wanted it to be given out, no more and no less than that. I think this is of vital importance, because They foresaw that the word, given through The Aetherius Society, in the way that They chose to give it, would go out to those people who were ready—not only to accept it, but even more important still—to ACT upon it.

The very reason that these two significant Transmissions were given through myself and released through The Aetherius Society is, in itself, the most definite pointer to our grave responsibilities in this coming clash between good and evil.

Some readers of this book may question the authenticity of these words as they would question the authenticity of anything they read. Others will "question" this authenticity for a different reason—in order to escape from the responsibility which these words place upon their shoulders.

I have never asked anyone to have a blind faith in anything—neither can I myself. My faith has to be built upon experience, logic and common sense. But many times has faith been tested in the fires of adversity. Never once have I regretted holding on, even apparently, according to my fallible mind, against basic logic—to my faith in the existence of the greater Beings and Their undoubted wisdom. All readers who are "non-believers" should adopt the same attitude, saying to themselves, after close study of these Transmissions, that such a thing is possible and it may be probable. Therefore—even though there be one chance in a thousand of it being correct—so vital is the advice in these Transmissions, that it should be acted upon in a definite manner. I can guarantee that if you adopt this attitude, very shortly you will have these words proven to you in a startling manner—beyond all shadow of all doubt.

Thousands of years ago seers labeled this present age "Kali Yuga", the age of the great conflict. The Bible talks about the "Armageddon", the bitter clash between the forces of darkness and the powers of Light.

The time of this clash is coming very shortly. In fact, it may even have started when you read this book.

Because Saint Goo-Ling and the Master Jesus gave the Transmissions when They did, as They did, through whom They chose, it is obvious that a certain result was desired by Them. As this is so, we can logically assume that no one will read this book by chance, but will be destined to do so. As far as you all are concerned this adds to the significance of the words herein, for you have been brought into contact with this truth for a good reason. One which you can turn to your lasting Karmic advantage if you re-dedicate your life in the light of the wisdom given herein.

To quote Saint Goo-Ling, ascended Master of the Great White Brotherhood: *"Listen with your very souls, for this is your hour and the opportunity will never be given again so prominently for 287 lives to come, as it is now."*

CHAPTER ONE

ANOTHER BLESSING BY THE MASTER JESUS

SAINT GOO-LING:

"Now at this time, the Being you knew as the Master Jesus will speak again and give another Blessing to the world. Sit still, close eyes and feel the release of Power which will be apparent to you as this Blessing is given.

"So important is this Blessing that, in future, it will become one of your prayers to be performed, at your Services, like the others.

"The Master Jesus has chosen a very strategic time to give this Blessing as you will soon hear for yourselves.

"Great forces are about to clash. Stupendous forces of darkness are preparing to bring about conditions on the surface of this world too horrible to contemplate. On the other hand, other forces have dedicated themselves to your protection. Very shortly these forces must clash in mortal combat and the prize of this combat is all humanoid life upon Earth.

"The prophecies are now being fulfilled.

"So it is on the verge of this that, once again, cometh the Master of Light—Jesus. He cometh even though you murdered Him. Even though you have turned against His word throughout the centuries. Even though you have scorned Him and some of your so-called mathematical minds have tried to prove His non-existence—He still comes. This demonstration of compassion is indeed the very essence of Spiritual devotion to a cause—and the cause is you.

"Be ye prepared to work for right—for this is the hour! The hour of the prophecies.

"The hour of the turning point of evolution, or the hour of the defeat of all which is good and Holy upon Earth.

"This is the hour.

"The hour of Light or darkness.

"The hour of Truth or lies.

"THE HOUR WHEN THE FOUNDATION STONES CAN BE LAID FOR THE NEW AGE OR NEVER CAN IT BE BUILT BY MAN UPON THIS PLANET.

"This is the crossroad of evolution. It is the beginning of greatness, or the beginning of darkness.

"It is the hour of Light, or a more stifling blackness than you have ever known before.

"You stand as helpless children in this hour.

"It is the hour when the Karmic book is written for each and everyone of you. When the Searchers look deep into your heart, your Soul and your environment and make Their judgment—yes judgment—accordingly.

"It is the hour of supreme triumph of all that is Glorious, or defeat of the best. The battlefield has been chosen. The armies are taking their terrible position.

"It is the hour of decision, for hereafter no man can stay on the sidelines. He is either a fighter for Spirituality or a slave of the darkest forces in the lowest hells.

"This is the hour when the prophecies are either proved right or wrong. Gird well your loins, prepare to stand fast for goodness so that the Light of evolution might remain a burning, bright flame and never be extinguished.

"This is the hour of decision into Spiritual action, or the hour of your fall because the opportunity has been missed.

"In this hour—for Those Who have come to help you in your

frightful struggle—comes Jesus again to Bless These Ones. Listen well. Listen with your very Souls, for this is your hour and the opportunity will never be given again so prominently for 287 lives to come as it is now.

"I go."

THE MASTER JESUS:

"Oh man, you came as a spark from God—through involution. Back to God you goeth—yet you choose the pathway, be it long and easy or short and hard.

"BLESSED ARE THE THREE ADEPTS, Who stand between you and your Spiritual defeat, at this time.

"Many centuries ago the Wise Ones looked into time and there They saw apparently inevitable results brought about by the fall of man. They conferred together, allowing the shining oil of sweet compassion to imbue Their negotiations. They took into consideration the deep Karmic implications of what was to come. Then turned They to Three devoted Beings and asked of These to give up the bliss of Their advanced Initiatory Status and take gross bodies, bound by Karma, held by the limitations of man and come and live and breathe and eat and pray and suffer among ye.

"The Three Adepts spent no time in consideration.

"Their Souls leapt within Them, filled with compassion for a people who were helpless against the might which threatened to crush them, even as a great hammer crushes a lowly stone. And so it was They came and throughout the years that They have been with you, They have fought your greatest and most important battles.

"Man, without the Three Adepts, you would have already been lost for a long, long time. Over and over again, these mighty Beings came to your rescue. When you stood helpless—They fought against tremendous odds for you. When you played in the garden of your simple ease—They sweat blood on your behalf. When you rolled in the pleasant, warm sunshine caring not—They suffered excruciating pain and agony for each and everyone of you.

"Indeed, oh God, indeed thrice Blessed are these Saviours of a whole planetary race.

"You stood as little, helpless children—by. Few of you even raised one hand in prayer, never mind your hearts, to help Those Who suffered for you. And yet, again and again and again and again, They stood and faced unbelievable odds on your behalf, for They cared for you. They loved you with a Love seldom shown by any other being to any other being.

"Seven times Blessed are the Three Adepts for Their greatness, for Their Love, for Their compassion, for the way They have helped a planetary race to remain sane, for the way that They have broken the bonds of slavery which—make no doubt about it—would, by now, have bound you tight to your wicked masters.

"Seven times Blessed are each one of these mighty Beings for the way that They have, despite your disbelief, despite your scorn, despite your treatment of Them, They have rallied and stood as a barrier between the human race and the depths of hell's hell.

"These are Blessed.

"These are Blessed in the minds of the greatest Masters in this System.

"These are Blessed in the minds of all good-thinking men, for if there be a man upon Earth who does not Bless These now—and yet knows of Their works—such a one as this has condemned himself to involution until his eyes be opened through painful experience.

"Blessed be the Three Adepts—now—for even again They stand between you and hell.

"It is, at this time, that those in the darker realms are waiting to spring their trap. For thousands of centuries they have planned this, carefully, move by move. Do you know man, not one single murderous dictator has been put into a position by chance? Conqueror after conqueror has been built by the dark ones to act as a recruiting agent upon the physical plane of your world! These have brought around them like wickedness and have taken this back to the lower realms with them, and have built the armies of evil there. It has been a plan cunningly conceived and you—the pawns in a game to gain a whole humanoid race. Did you know that man?

"I, Jesus, declare this to be, up till now, the secret of secrets.

"Now they wait for their 'armageddon'. Their schemes are laid; their plots worked out; their strategy computed. They wait to move and you stand as a lamb would stand before a hungry lion, helpless, defenseless, wrapped up, involved by your own wrong thought and action, you stand—if you know—quaking.

"But between you and the others stand Three Glorious Lights.

"Three Lights—brilliant Lights, Lights of strength, Lights of power, Lights of knowledge and ability gained in the hardest schools of life.

"Three Lights of Service.

"Three Lights of God. Yes, Three Lights of God bearing the swords of Karma, protected by the armour of Their complete Spiritual dedication to God's Cause.

"Blessed are the Three Adepts!

"THESE THREE HAVE DONE MORE FOR THE HUMAN RACE UPON EARTH THAN ANY OTHER THREE MASTERS WHO HAVE EVER CONTACTED THE HUMAN RACE AT ANY TIME UPON THIS PLANET.

"In comparison with what They have done for you, my task and the results of what I did were naught, were not even worthy of mention! I, Jesus, whom you murdered and who rose again to prove to you a great Spiritual Truth, have made this declaration before my God!

"This is Truth!

"Indeed, indeed Blessed are These Ones.

"They should always be Blessed by each and everyone of

you. Never should a day pass but what you Bless These. You should devote your whole life in Service to These, for by serving Them, you serve all men—and vastly more important than this—you serve the Karmic Gods.

"At this time may the great Spiritual Flame of protection surround These Three.

"I Bless Them with all my heart, with all my Soul.

"I BLESS THEM WITH ALL MY SPIRIT.

(Jesus intoned a mystical Mantra of Power Invocation.)

"I now invoke a Power for and on behalf of the Three Lights.

(A further intoning of a mystical Power Mantra followed.)

"Blessed are the Three Adepts for what They are about to do.

"So endeth this Blessing.

"Oh adorable children, be strong at this time. Reach upwards and inwards to the Light which shineth there, then come outwards dedicated in Spiritual service to all and you will never regret this step.

"Oh Divine and Wondrous Spirit,
Oh Everlasting Lord of Supreme Hosts,
We pray, at this time, that Your unquenchable Light,
That the Power of Your compassion illuminates and protects
The Three Adepts in Their greatest trial.
Oh Divine and Wondrous God,
May They succeed in Their Mission.
May They save helpless humanity from the monsters,
Which it has created.
Oh Mighty God,
Give us all the strength to stand, unflinchingly,
By the side of These,
So that a Spiritual Triumph might be born upon Earth.

Oh Divine Father of all Wondrous Creation,
We raise our minds to You—now,
Requesting that Your Power may fall upon the heads,
And penetrate the hearts of all men.
So that they may be stronger in their Spiritual purpose.
So that they may live and act in the Light of God knowledge,
Forever and forever.

"I came, at this time, to Bless the Three and to tell you all of these things.

"May you be guided by your Spirit.

"Oh little children, become fully grown by acting upon these things, then will you:

                GO WITH GOD."

CHAPTER TWO

THE TRUTHS OF SAINT GOO-LING

Saint Goo-Ling is an ascended Master of the Great White Brotherhood. He has lived upon this Earth for over two thousand years in His physical body, which has passed through the Initiation of Ascension. (Note 1.) His major task is that of keeping the Seal for the Great White Brotherhood. This makes Him one of the most prominent Members of the terrestrial Hierarchal Order. Saint Goo-Ling has been communicating through myself for about 12 years. As you will see, this is not a new communication by any means. It was Saint Goo-Ling Who introduced the Master Jesus when "The Twelve Blessings" were delivered by Jesus, between July 27th, 1958 and October 12th, 1958. Even before this time, Saint Goo-Ling was communicating His wisdom through me and never once, naturally, during all this time, have we found the words of this Master to be anything but the gospel truth.

It is fitting for a Master of Cosmic Status like Jesus, born as He was on the Planet Venus, to be introduced by a Master of the terrestrial Hierarchy before He speaks to Earth. This brings about a certain Karmic balance to the powers released by the great speech, delivered by the Master Jesus, printed herein.

In case some of you, unfamiliar with the approach of the Master Saint Goo-Ling, should feel that He is maybe over exaggerating, may I state here quite definitely that this is not His way at all. In fact, like most Masters, He is a master of understatement and certainly not one of overstatement of any facts. Therefore, His words must be taken in the most serious way possible to you.

"Now at this time, the Being you knew as the Master Jesus will speak again and will give another Blessing to the world. Sit still, close eyes and feel the release of Power which will be apparent to you as this Blessing is given."

There was no doubt about a release of power felt during the Blessing given by the Master Jesus. All who attended the live Transmission in Los Angeles and those who heard the tape recording of this Blessing in the London Headquarters of the Society, felt this tremendous power release which was brought about by Jesus as He gave this magnificent Blessing. In fact, so impressed were some Members in London that, after they had heard the Blessing, they instructed the Secretary of the Society—Reginald Holdaway—to ring me up personally and try to convey to me some of their feelings of deep gratitude. That they felt the powers released, there was no doubt.

Members and sympathizers, who attended the live Transmission at the Los Angeles Headquarters, also expressed their feelings, which were most affected by, not only the words of the Master, but the almost overwhelming power of His wonderful Love which pervaded them as this Transmission was being delivered.

"So important is this Blessing that, in the future, it will become one of your prayers to be performed, at your Services, like the others."

All attenders, familiar with The Aetherius Society, know that the Service of "The Twelve Blessings" is performed during all Magnetization Periods, Divine and Healing Services. All those of you who have taken part in pilgrimages to the Holy Mountains also know that "The Twelve Blessings", as given by the Master Jesus, are performed on these Mountains. Therefore, it is not surprising that Saint Goo-Ling, here, has given us the directive to include this Blessing in all of our future Divine Services, special Power Circles, Healing Services and pilgrimages. (Note 2.)

"The Master Jesus has chosen a very strategic time to give this Blessing as you will soon hear for yourselves.

"Great forces are about to clash. Stupendous forces of darkness are preparing to bring about conditions on the surface of this world too horrible to contemplate. On the other hand, other forces have dedicated themselves to your protection. Very shortly these forces must clash in mortal combat and the prize of this combat is all humanoid life upon Earth."

This is a statement with stupendous implications. Please note what I said previously, Saint Goo-Ling never has been guilty of an overstatement of fact! He is a balanced Master and One of understatement. When a Master of His calibre states: *"Stupendous forces of darkness are preparing to bring about conditions on the surface of this world too horrible to contemplate"*, He means just that.

There is no doubt, whatever, that this is the most significant time in the history of the human race.

It is the time when the turning point has been reached. Mankind can no longer be permitted, by Karmic Law, to stray as blatantly from the paths of truth as he has done throughout his past lives. Sooner or later the forces "behind" mankind had to come into conflict. All philosophers who think deeply enough must agree that, "behind" the human race, there are forces for good and evil; that as a man thinks, so is he. If he thinks evil, then the forces of evil can use him as a pawn. In the Transmission by the Master Jesus we will examine a direct statement, made by Jesus, to this effect.

The present can be pictured in this way. Imagine, if you can, a great army of intelligences lined up, not in physical bodies as you know physical bodies, but bodies even more physical and gross than your physical body, yet more easily directed by thought pressures. This army is on the lower astral realms of Earth. The leaders of this army are able, not only to control their armed forces in the lower astral realms, but, as we will see later, continually fill their ranks with recruits whom they have specially prepared on the physical planes of Earth. On the other hand, there are Three Individuals lined up against this stupendous might of evil. Probably these Three Individuals may even be supplemented by Two more Adepts, making a total of Five for this coming conflict.

As Saint Goo-Ling states: *"Very shortly these forces must clash in mortal combat and the prize of this combat is all humanoid life upon Earth."*

Once the move is made against these evil forces by the Five Adepts, then the Adepts are committed, by Karmic Law, to continue with Their action to the very end. There will be no turning back! For, were They to turn back after once starting, the evil forces would see the possibility of the defeat of the Adepts and overrun the mind belt of the physical plane in a very short time. So powerful are these evil forces, so deep their concentrative abilities, that mankind would not stand a chance against the tremendous mental pressures put upon him by these entities. He would be mentally enslaved within a very short time and, once this had happened, never would the evil entities give up their position as dictators; never would they allow their slaves, the human race, to regain their freedom. Once they were committed to move there would be no turning back for them, either. So that, when the conflict does start, indeed the prize will be the freedom of all humanoid life upon Earth, at least as far as the evil ones are concerned.

It must be remembered that evil intelligences on the lower astral realms cannot be bribed by wealth, as we know it on this Earth. If they want jewels, they can think them into being. If they wish a gold castle, especially on a non-permanent basis, they can bring this into being by thought. It is power which can bribe them. This, too, can be brought into being by thought, but the challenge is much greater than thinking together a sapphire, or a bar of platinum. They live, not so much as you do on air, liquid, food and love but, on hate and suffering. The vibrations released by the suffering of mankind during a war, for instance, are nourishment to these sadistic vampires. Therefore, they bring about their most cherished delicacies, their virtual food, by causing division, hatred, suffering and strife upon Earth.

It is obvious that, since the Initiation of Earth on July 8th, 1964, so much tremendous power is now latent in the Earth—Herself, that the leaders of the dark forces must be getting very worried in case this power should be suddenly released and such a release cause their disintegration and rebirth in terrible limitations upon another world, where they would be so limited for thousands of lives that they could not enjoy their present position of sadistical power ever again. In the light of this knowledge will they act and fight as never they have fought before. (Note 3.)

"The prophecies are now being fulfilled.

"So it is on the verge of this that, once again, cometh the Master of Light—Jesus. He cometh even though you murdered Him. Even though you have turned against His word throughout the centuries. Even though you have scorned Him and some of your so-called mathematical minds have tried to prove His non-existence—He still comes. This demonstration of compassion is indeed the very essence of Spiritual devotion to a cause—and the cause is you."

Saint Goo-Ling here states that it is on the verge of the direct action by the dark forces that the Master Jesus returned at this time. Even though He came two thousand years ago and was ill-treated by mankind, who even in those days were used as pawns by the black ones to bring about His murder, He nevertheless forgives those responsible—to return again, at the turning point in the history of mankind. Saint Goo-Ling describes this forgiveness as a demonstration of compassion which is the very essence of Spiritual devotion to a cause. Indeed it is this.

Picture, if you can, the saintly Jesus Who came to help mankind. Who came, not to forgive you your sins, for such a thing is impossible in Karmic Law, but Who came to teach you the way to peace, harmony, love and brotherhood. Who came to rescue terrestrial man from his misery, despair and ignorance. Picture such a Being as this crucified by an uncouth, ignorant rabble—alone on the cross with but a few followers scattered in the crowd. Indeed a tragic picture, one that would bring tears to the eyes of the strongest among us. And that is how it was. Yet, despite this ill-treatment, He has come again to Earth many times throughout the centuries, in many different ways. And He came just recently and gave you "The Twelve Blessings"—great Spiritual teachings which have meant so much to ALL those who have practised them. Even again He came, in what can virtually be described as the darkest hour ever faced by the human race since it has been on this Planet. Indeed is such compassion as His beyond the common understanding and appreciation of fallible terrestrial man. But then, this is the quality of compassion which makes the Master Jesus—Immortal.

"Be ye prepared to work for right—for this is the hour! The hour of the prophecies."

In this statement the Master directs all to be prepared to work for those things which are right, good and true. He does not and could not, in this Transmission, go into the details of these things for you have already been given these. All Members of The Aetherius Society and those who have studied our literature have, throughout the past eleven years, been given directions over and over again by the Cosmic Masters, in precise detail, of the right action to take in all terrestrial situations. The teachings given by these Beings have obviously been specially designed so that when your hour came—and it has come—you would know how to act and to what cause to devote your life.

"The hour of the turning point of evolution, or the hour of the defeat of all which is good and Holy upon Earth."

If the Cosmic Adepts should be defeated by the massive armies of the lower astral realms, the results would be the same as a defeat of all which is Holy upon Earth. This does not mean to say, of course, that the Three or Five Adepts are the only Beings good and Holy upon Earth—not at all. But it means that, if the Adepts should fall in this coming conflict, then the dark forces would be able to crush all that is good and Holy upon Earth by direct mental and physical attacks upon the human race. So restricted is man, because of his limited thought and action throughout the centuries, that he would not stand any chance against such overwhelming odds. In fact, he would fall right into their evil trap. If, for instance, the dark forces wanted to conquer the globe, they could do so by causing a certain country to release atomic missiles on other countries. The countries attacked would retaliate by further missile bombardment and before long—what?

The world in chaos!

Blindness and disease as rulers!

Famine, caused by great stretches of land being fouled by radio-activity, would be the aftermath of atomic madness.

Later would come gross and ghastly mutations. Things born which would no longer resemble the humanoid body as you know it today would roam the surface of the globe. Some of them, diabolically strong, carnivorous, would destroy all flesh, both human and animal, that they could find. Then, from that stage it would be easy for the dark forces to concentrate upon mind after mind and mold them into the pattern which they wanted; to learn all they could from them; to treat them as robot thinking machines, feeding them with only that information they wanted them to have so that they could work for them and add to their power and evil accomplishments throughout the coming centuries.

All of you will admit that it would be quite easy and certainly possible for the dark forces to take over this Earth in the way mentioned, and this is one of the ways they would do it with the least effort to themselves. A concentrated thought in the right direction would release an atomic missile. This missile would cause the release of others and an atomic war would lay waste a civilization as we know it. Then could they act and be guaranteed of terrible success---!

Some people, who have suffered orthodox conditioning when they were younger, may state that God would not "allow" such a horrible thing to happen. God supposedly "allowed" the concentration camps in Germany and the murder of millions of Jews. God did not stop the atom bombs being dropped on Nagasaki and Hiroshima, causing tens of thousands of Japanese to be killed and thousands of ghastly mutations to be born throughout the last decade because of this. It is not God Which "allows" these things or brings them about.

IT IS MAN WHO ALLOWS THEM.

It is man who not only allowed the murder of the Jews by the evil nazis, but—in certain cases—actually helped in this vile sadism.

God is Law.

Nothing can operate outside of this Law, because nothing is stronger than the Absolute Creator—Itself. But if man, born with certain freewill, wishes to mold the pattern of his life in one direction, he is allowed to do this, at least for a certain time. The black magicians were not stopped from becoming black magicians by any intervention from the Absolute. As long as they obeyed certain laws, then they were allowed to become black magicians for a certain time. There is always that limitation upon it.

Evolution seems to be the only path which goes on indefinitely. Involution cannot last because there seems to be a time when the Law intervenes, as it has done in the past through the Three Adepts Who were put here by the Karmic Law and Who operate strictly within its confines. No power is greater than the Karmic Law and all powers are governed by it. Thus there comes an end to involution.

If the Three Adepts are successful in Their next Mission,

this will NOT mean that every dark force on the lower astral realms will have been defeated and mankind will be able to go forward without any astral interference for the rest of his days. Far from it! But it will mean that a significant defeat of the dark forces will be brought about to stop the present action, which the demoniac forces have planned for centuries and which is due to be put into operation in the next few weeks---!

The Three Adepts are also preparing the way for the coming of the Next Great Avatar to Earth. This is a major aspect of the Cosmic Plan, but the Coming—whenever it may be—cannot take place until favourable results are brought about by the Karmic Mission of the Three.

We should all thank God that there are Beings like the Three Adepts willing to take upon Themselves such vast responsibilities—should we not?

"This is the hour.
"The hour of Light or darkness.
"The hour of Truth or lies.
"THE HOUR WHEN THE FOUNDATION STONES CAN BE LAID FOR THE NEW AGE OR NEVER CAN IT BE BUILT BY MAN UPON THIS PLANET."

Many of you are undoubtedly familiar with the mass of Metaphysical literature which is being published, just lately, about the New Age. Most of these publications seem to give the impression that the New Age will be built easily by man and, thereafter, he will enjoy tax- and work-free conditions for the rest of his lives. Dear readers, the New Age has to be earned.

The New Age has to be built by sweat and toil and Spiritual dedication.

The New Age will be the foundation of the true enlightenment of mankind and therefore must be built by the enlightened.

The New Age will not be a respecter of persons, colour, class, creed or even religious beliefs for that matter.

Throughout the past few years, the Master Aetherius has repeatedly told us that the New Age will be built by those Spiritual pioneers with courage, determination and complete loyalty and devotion to the cause of Truth and Spirituality—not by the armchair theorists, or by the "baby-patting" emotionalists—far from it.

Here, a Member of the Hierarchal Order on this Earth—not an earthman's opinion this—states quite plainly that, should the coming conflict be lost by the Forces of Light, then the foundation stones can never be laid for the New Age by man upon this Planet.

In order to fully appreciate the meaning of this vital statement, it must be realized, firstly, that the Three Adepts CAN LOSE this battle! When They go into the lower astral realms, They do so with a limitation imposed upon Them by the Karmic pattern of mankind. They go into the lower astral realms with only a part of Their Super-consciousness, centered in Themselves, as it were. In other words, They do not operate in full "Cosmic Aspect". Were They to be able to make Their sorties in full "Cosmic Aspect", these would not last long and the results could be guaranteed to be successful. But such would be a Divine intervention, the like of which mankind has not earned at this time. So therefore, the Three Adepts are definitely operating under gross limitation, imposed upon Them by the Law, because of the Karmic pattern of mankind. They are taking tremendous risks and undoubtedly suffering great pain, because of the limitations imposed upon Them by the actions of mankind. Such action denotes a depth of compassion above terrestrial understanding or appreciation.

The Three Adepts have proven Their capabilities in this field; proven Their compassionate feelings towards mankind many, many times in the past. (Note 4.) So therefore, let us not delude ourselves into believing that, because the Three Adepts are fighting your battles for you, They are guaranteed of success. I only wish to God that this were the case!

After carefully planning Their moves and taking action, They are committed to every move They are able to make in the direction specifically laid down by Their Karmic assignment. If They should not get the backing that They need—the power, prayers, love, from YOU—and should They lose this battle, it will mean that the dark forces will take the action already described. This will cause global war. In this case then, mankind will be released from his physical structure to be reborn upon a more primitive world and, therefore, will have to start again after being retarded hundreds of lifetimes. He will have to work his way back to the position he is in now and will have to rebuild for himself a New Age upon this more primitive Planet. If he is able to do this, in the face of his previous defeat by the dark forces, he will then have to prove to the Karmic Lords that he is worthy of the inheritance of this Planet—Earth. This is the implication behind that very important statement by Saint Goo-Ling.

A truth which dwarfs all other truths in your life, bar none.

Later on in this explanation, a detailed account will be given of what you can do, on your own behalf, to help the Three Adepts.

"This is the crossroads of evolution. It is the beginning of greatness, or the beginning of darkness.

"It is the hour of Light, or a more stifling blackness than you have ever known before."

If the battle is won by the Three or Five Adepts, with all the help you can humanly give to Them, then a great Age of Light will gradually dawn upon this Earth.

If the battle is lost by the Three Adepts, this will lead to the darkest hour that mankind has ever known.

"You stand as helpless children in this hour.

"It is the hour when the Karmic book is written for each and everyone of you. When the Searchers look deep into your heart, your Soul and your environment and make Their judgment—yes judgment—accordingly."

It is in the darkest hours that the greatest Spiritual opportunities are offered. The Master Saint Goo-Ling reminds us that it is in these hours of our greatest opportunity that our greatest Karma will be incurred, either on the positive or on the negative side. Every thought and action of man is recorded, either to his credit or debit. If he owes more than he has paid, then he is indeed in Karmic debt. After these Transmissions, which have stated the case so perfectly, if those people acquainted with these Truths do not act upon them to the very best of their ability, then they stand a chance of incurring a Karmic debt, which reflects directly upon the position they will find themselves in during future lives to come. If, on the other hand, they devote their whole lives, in view of the vast importance of these Transmissions, to helping the Three Adepts in the numerous ways detailed later, then they will be judged accordingly and great must their reward be throughout all future lives!

"It is the hour of supreme triumph of all that is Glorious, or defeat of the best. The battlefield has been chosen. The armies are taking their terrible position."

The battlefield will be the lower astral realms—the hells.

The armies, on the one hand, will constitute the essence of evil and, on the other hand, either the Three or the Five Adepts Who, despite Their small numbers, have great prowess.

"It is the hour of decision, for hereafter no man can stay on the sidelines. He is either a fighter for Spirituality or a slave of the darkest forces in the lowest hells."

Here we have another very definite statement made by Saint Goo-Ling. The Masters have seen fit to give this information through The Aetherius Society because They obviously have seen that certain people—who will not obtain this book by chance but by design—are vitally needed and can play a very important part in this coming conflict. After reading this book and also the last

Transmission by the Master Aetherius, no longer can anyone stay on the sidelines, but must join in to help if they have one ounce of Spiritual decency within them. (Note 5.) If this opportunity is missed, then they put themselves so far back that they are liable to become prone to astral realm enslavement. This is a frightful thought—one I only wish to God I had not the job of telling you. But I have that job. It is my mission to put this out in plain, cold, unadulterated, straight-forward truth to you. So therefore I would be failing my Masters and you were I to do otherwise.

A great opportunity is given to ALL of you who read these things. Whatever you do, dear readers—whatever you do—please do not pass up this opportunity if there is one million-to-one chance in your own mind of its being correct. If you feel, as most Members will, that it is correct, then for your sake and the sake of humanity do not miss this vital opportunity for, if you do miss it, you will regret it for lives to come.

In case some of you may believe that you are unable to help because you do not have the ability, may I again state quite definitely that everyone reading these words can help. It is your duty to do so in the light of this Transmission.

"This is the hour when the prophecies are either proved right or wrong. Gird well your loins, prepare to stand fast for goodness so that the Light of evolution might remain a burning, bright flame and never be extinguished.

"This is the hour of decision into Spiritual action, or the hour of your fall because the opportunity has been missed."

Here again the Master Goo-Ling makes it quite plain that He is giving a great opportunity to ALL who come into contact with His Words. He also makes it plain that your fall is inevitable if you miss this opportunity. This is a test for everyone. If you fail, you cannot rise to a higher classroom without lives of painful experience. If you pass this test, then you WILL rise to a higher classroom and nothing can stop this magnificent rise.

"In this hour—for Those Who have come to help you in your frightful struggle—comes Jesus again to Bless These Ones. Listen well. Listen with your very Souls, for this is your hour and the opportunity will never be given again so prominently for 287 lives to come as it is now.

"I go."

It is on the verge of the Mission of the Three Adepts, in fact the main reason for Their presence on Earth at this time, that the Master Jesus came on September the 23rd to give a Blessing to Them and to release His majestic Power and Love to these Beings upon Whom the freedom and sanity of a whole Planet depends.

The Master Goo-Ling states here, again quite plainly, that if you miss this opportunity to help—in the ways detailed—you will never again be given an opportunity as potentially Spiritually great as this for the next 287 lives.

This definite number of 287 lives, by the way, is like the rest of the quotation given here by Saint Goo-Ling—an exact figure. It is not an earthman's guess or a mathematician's estimation. It is an exact figure given by a Being from the terrestrial Hierarchy, Who has had an opportunity—during the past 2000 years—to study the Akashic Records and work out the logical implications of them.

Ladies and gentlemen, 287 lives can be a long, long time.

I think that this last illustration of Truth should teach you, better than anything else, the importance of your cooperation and determination to help Those Who have come to save you—Those Who will suffer any pain in order to do so.

CHAPTER THREE

THE TRUTHS OF JESUS

"Oh man, you came as a spark from God—through involution. Back to God you goeth—yet you choose the pathway, be it long and easy or short and hard."

In the beginning all was Perfection. There was but the Absolute and nothing else. Then, for some reason best known to Itself, the Divine Principle saw fit to involve Itself in Creation. It placed the involved part of Itself—Creation—in a matrix of energy, governed by strict Laws and caused all life throughout all the Worlds to come into being. In some cases this life evolved from simple forms into complex and sophisticated creatures. As the physical evolved, so did the mental abilities of these life forms evolve, until they were able to manipulate the energy matrix, by obedience to the Laws which govern it, to such an extent that they learned to become self-conscious beings. Gradually, this self-consciousness is being evolved through experience plane after experience plane, until it will, eventually, go back to its Source again, namely—the Divine Principle from Which all came. (Note 6.)

The statement, above, made by the Master Jesus, is, as you would expect, Metaphysically correct in all ways. When a life form has reached a stage of self-consciousness, it is then able to choose, by applied reasoning, whether it will speed up its evolution back to its original Source and thereby take the hard path, or whether it will lengthen out this span through almost infinite time and take the long, much easier course back to the original Divine Source from Which it came.

Although terrestrial man is the most involved and least sophisticated humanoid life form in this Solar System he, nevertheless, has reached the stage of self-consciousness which enables him to choose the path which he will take through his evolution. It is a certain fact that there are many systems of progression, which have been evolved upon Earth through the centuries, which are specially designed to speed up the path taken through experience by the self-conscious individual. All of the best Yoga systems do this.

Up until even a relatively short time ago, the systems of isolation of the individual from the masses, if strictly adhered to and the recommended exercises practised with single-minded diligence, brought about a speeding up of evolution, because of heightened sensitivity and enhanced awareness and knowledge brought about within the individual by pressures on subtle nerve ganglia exerted by these exercises. Energies, latent within the mento-physical structure of man, can be, with certain occult practices, released so as to bring about the deeper mental states such as Contemplation and Meditation. The latter state, especially, is one which does enhance the pattern and velocity of man's travel through the planes of evolution. There are other states above this which allow the individual to break away from the necessary experience cycle, called rebirth, in this terrestrial classroom and travel to more highly evolved Planets so that the experience of the individual can be greatly enhanced, and the knowledge and awareness developed into a wisdom essential to the higher aspects of man's journey back to his Divine Source. (Note 1.)

On the other hand, mankind, having developed his self-consciousness, can choose, if he wishes, a longer path through his experience cycles by taking life easy and enjoying all the luxuries which were invented by his intelligence as it became more sophisticated.

So much freedom has mankind got in his own pattern of evolution, that he is even able to retard it and to set himself back upon the path—which many do by committing crimes, even though they have been told many times that such deeds would hold up their progress.

We are now in the Aquarian Age. The Age of service to the masses. No longer are the systems of isolation recommended by the true Teachers. As a matter of fact—like it or not and some of us may not like it—the systems now recommended in this Age, or in this stage of the evolution of mankind as a unit, are just the opposite from isolationism. The Aquarian Age, with its emphasis on improvement of the conditions for the mass of humanity, demands the metaphysician to spend his time in service among men rather than isolating himself from mankind as he has been recommended to do throughout the past centuries in order to enjoy personal bliss. As the Aquarian experience cycle advances, more and more emphasis will be placed upon service in order to improve the educational systems and living conditions of the majority.

At this time, we are reminded by the Master Jesus that we can either indulge ourselves and thereby hold up our evolutionary journey towards our precious Source, or we can serve mankind and so speed this journey up. The man who holds up his evolution is indeed the biggest of all fools for sooner or later like a flame pointing upwards, he too must reach for the Spiritual Heavens above and begin his hard climb back. It is innate in the nature of all sentient beings to do this, for all sentient beings are involved particles of the original Perfection. They were sent on a journey through experience, outwards from the Source and it was predetermined by the Source, even before they were sent outwards, that each particle would travel "home" again into the Absolute Womb from which it sprung. Any straying from this is a deviation from the predetermination of the Absolute Designer in the beginning and can only be of a temporary nature. Sooner or later, no matter how involved each particle has become, it must start to evolve itself. This is one of the inevitabilities of Creation. Coupled with this fact is that specially designed energy impulses are bombarding the whole Solar System at this particular time during the

Aquarian Age. This makes the inner yearning of all self-conscious creatures so much more acute. So acute, in fact, that in his striving to evolve man will bring about in the next 2000 years the greatest Spiritual renaissance ever seen on this Planet, if the Three Adepts are successful in the performance of Their assignment.

The journey back to the Source is inevitable. It is up to each self-conscious individual to pick the time when they start this journey in real earnest.

"BLESSED ARE THE THREE ADEPTS, Who stand between you and your Spiritual defeat, at this time."

The main reason for the Transmission, by the Master Jesus, was to give a Blessing and to release power to the Three Adepts, Who are Interplanetary Beings introduced into Earth physical structures so that They may perform a vital Mission on behalf of terrestrial man. (Note 4.)

"Many centuries ago the Wise Ones looked into time and there They saw apparently inevitable results brought about by the fall of man. They conferred together, allowing the shining oil of sweet compassion to imbue Their negotiations. They took into consideration the deep Karmic implications of what was to come."

This statement obviously refers to an action taken by the Hierarchal Lords of this Solar System. It is phrased in an interesting fashion. You will note that Jesus states here: *"...the Wise Ones looked into time..."* and not: *"...the Wise Ones looked into the future."* There is a subtle difference and a pointed one, in some ways, between the inferences of the two statements. It is almost as though we are being told that the Hierarchal Lords were not only Space Travellers, but Time Travellers as well. Hence, Their ability to examine time, for the Master goes on to say: *"...They saw apparently inevitable results brought about by the fall of man"*, and not: *"...They saw inevitable results to be brought about by the fall of man."*

It would appear, from a preliminary examination of the text, that the Wise Ones were able to ascertain exactly those things which had already happened and yet could be altered, because of the time level of Their point of reference in comparison with the time level of the point of reference of the happening. In other words, we could possibly describe it thus—everything is happening in the—Now. In the—Now, the particle has been set forth and in the—Now, the particle has passed through hundreds of millions of lives of experience, through tens of thousands of experience cycles in different universal classrooms and in the—Now, the particle is returning, or truer still, has returned to the Source.

The inference in the statement by the Master Jesus gives, upon consideration, a deeper appreciation of the—Now—of all things.

To sum up, then, the Hierarchal Lords were able to make an exact assessment of conditions which would be brought about by the fall of man, engineered by the mental enslavement of the human race by certain power-seeking, sadistic and Spiritually involved beings on the lower astral realms of this Planet. It was when They saw this, that They decided to take definite action against it.

"Then turned They to Three devoted Beings and asked of These to give up the bliss of Their advanced Initiatory Status and take gross bodies, bound by Karma, held by the limitations of man and come and live and breathe and eat and pray and suffer among ye.

"The Three Adepts spent no time in consideration.

"Their Souls leapt within Them, filled with compassion for a people who were helpless against the might which threatened to crush them, even as a great hammer crushes a lowly stone. And so it was They came and throughout the years that They have been with you, They have fought your greatest and most important battles."

The Great Lords took into consideration the Karmic implications of any action They may have to take in order to relieve the situation They foresaw. After such consideration, They then, as the Master Jesus states quite plainly, consulted Three Individuals Who appeared to be equipped to deal with the situation. Even though these Three Individuals, because of Their Initiatory Status, were obviously in positions allowed by such evolution, They did not hesitate to take upon Themselves the gross limitation which inhabitation of a terrestrial body would impose. So filled with compassion were They for a people who would become helpless against the mental ingenuity of stronger forces, that They accepted the assignment and—what must have been to such evolved Beings— the misery and privation imposed by the limitations of a gross physical structure.

Even though you may be an animal lover, there are very few who would, if requested, inhabit the body of a monkey so that you could live with monkeys, eat and sleep with them in order to help the monkey world. The Three Adepts made a choice which is just as different—probably even more so—as this from Their preassigned environment. Unlike the man who might devote his life, *as a man,* to looking after monkeys, the Three Adepts had to inhabit gross bodies in order to be allowed, by Karmic Law, to intervene in those things which—as far as we are concerned—are due to happen. The fact that little time was spent by Them in consideration should give readers some small idea of Their true compassion for helpless mankind.

In the same statement Jesus makes the point that They came and, throughout the years, have fought the greatest and most important battles on behalf of mankind. The Aetherius Society has dozens of tape recordings, delivered by the Master Aetherius, Who has given complete move by move accounts of the mighty work done to-date by the Three Adepts. Each of these assignments, graphically described as they are, would fill a full-sized book in itself.

Only a small fraction of what the Three have already done for mankind to-date has yet been published. (Note 4.)

"Man, without the Three Adepts, you would have already been lost for a long, long time. Over and over again, these mighty Beings came to your rescue. When you stood helpless—They fought against tremendous odds for you. When you played in the garden of your simple ease—They sweat blood on your behalf. When you rolled in the pleasant, warm sunshine caring not—They suffered excruciating pain and agony for each and everyone of you.

"Indeed, oh God, indeed thrice Blessed are the Saviours of a whole planetary race."

As some explanation of what the Master meant by the last sentence is necessary, a very brief resume of what the Three Adepts have done for mankind, since February 1960, is well worthy of your study.

SORTIES BY THE THREE ADEPTS INTO THE LOWER ASTRAL REALMS OF EARTH

PERIOD: February 1960 to January 1966.
NUMBER OF SORTIES: 38.
CATEGORIES: 4 — A, B, C, D.

CATEGORY A: 7 sorties. Transmutation of powerful centres of evil which gave rise to people like hitler, nero, napoleon, attila, etc.
CATEGORY B: 6 sorties. Scientific centres with advanced scientific knowledge, such as: making of hydrogen bombs, atomic experimentation, development of disease spores for bacteriological warfare to attack the physical plane of Earth.
CATEGORY C: 3 sorties. Transmutation of powerful black magicians who operated some of the most powerful centres of evil.
CATEGORY D: 27 Phases—22 sorties. Special Assignment. *Eviction of the alien intelligence from the lower astral realms.*
THREE DISTINCT PHASES: *1)The Challenge:* 5 sorties. The Three Adepts fight the righthand man of the alien intelligence,

an "advanced" black magician of great powers.

2)The alien: 11 sorties. Strategic battles and final eviction of the alien intelligence from the lower astral realms and out of this Solar System.

3)The Fortress: 6 sorties. Final battles and transmutation of the black magician who acted under the mental control of the android and was brought back into the lower realms, even after he had been transmuted by the Three Adepts in a previous phase of the operation. This may give you a small idea of the powers of the android or alien.

SORTIE BY ADEPT NUMBER ONE
INTO THE LOWER ASTRAL REALMS OF EARTH

In April 1959, Adept Number One fought a very powerful black magician, who was one of the dark ones who caused the murder of the Master Jesus. After a very bitter battle, the black magician was transmuted. However, *Adept Number One was Himself killed during the action.* He was brought back to life in answer to His appeal to remain in a terrestrial body so that His vital Mission to Earth could be accomplished.

THE THREE ADEPTS TAKE PART IN AN INTER-GALACTIC CONFLICT, WHICH WAS CALLED– "THE BATTLE OF GOTHA"

PERIOD: From March 29th, 1966 to March 24th, 1967.
NUMBER OF SORTIES: 16.

Total number of Sorties into the hells by the Three Adepts: 55.

SPECIAL POWER TRANSMISSIONS

As well as performing the Sorties of Karmic Transmutation against the lower astral regions, the Three Adepts were also used by Cosmic Intelligences in a number of Special Power Transmissions, each of which was vital to the welfare of the human race.

Brief details of these assignments are given below.

Each one of these Special Power Transmissions has been, in its own way, completely unique. Between 1957 and 1966, the Three Adepts participated in a total of 92 Special Power Transmissions. Listed below are the principle types of Power Transmissions given during that period with an example of each type. This classification is, at best, very general and serves to illustrate the extremely broad and versatile capabilities of the Three Adepts.

Special Power Transmissions, "Standard Type"...............................40
Power Transmissions Using Basic Cooperators in Blocks..............12
Jupiterean Series.. 8
Operation World Healing..12
November 1964 Emergency... 3
Emergency During The Special Mission.. 1
Operation One One One (prior to July 8th, 1964)............................14
Operation One One One (after July 8th, 1964).................................. 1
The Cosmic Initiation Of Earth.. 1

                        total number given............. 92

SPECIAL POWER TRANSMISSIONS, "STANDARD" TYPE:

On October 22nd, 1962, when the United States of America and the Soviet Union stood in dangerous confrontation over the presence of Russian atomic missiles based in Cuba, a Special Power Transmission was given through the Three Adepts, beginning at 8:40 p.m. and ending at 10:30 p.m. Tremendous Spiritual energies were radiated through the Three Adepts by Mars Sector 6 from Satellite Number 3, to balance a condition which threatened to plunge the world into war. Within a month the Cuban crisis had ended in a nervous peace with the withdrawal of the Soviet missiles and the lifting of the American naval blockade. The strain of this Transmission on the Three Adepts was so acute that Mars Sector 6 ordered Them to take extreme care of Their mental and physical structures.

This was but one of 40 Special Transmissions of Spiritual Power through the Three Adepts to preserve mankind from all-out war, disease, famine or other terrible results of man's wrong thought and action.

POWER TRANSMISSIONS USING BASIC COOPERATORS:

On August 26th, 1963, from 9:00 p.m. until 9:47 p.m., a Special Power Manipulation was given through the Three Adepts, the Great White Brotherhood and through basic terrestrial cooperators to saturate all levels of terrestrial consciousness with Spiritual energies. Faithful and devoted Members of The Aetherius Society, who had been notified that a Special Power Transmission would be held and who attended in blocks throughout the world, were actually used as channels for energy which was poured through them according to their individual capacities. Afterward a Special Karmic Manipulation was held on behalf of all basic cooperators who attended this Transmission and who had proved their loyalty to The Aetherius Society and what it stands for.

This Divine opportunity for active participation, as well as the Karmic Manipulation which followed on this occasion, was made possible by the presence of the Three Adepts upon Earth. Altogether, 12 Transmissions of this type have been given.

JUPITERIAN SERIES, EMERGENCY POWER TRANSMISSIONS:

On February 6th, 1962, at 9:00 p.m., came the most important Power Transmission ever held for the benefit of terrestrial man, up to that time. Spiritual energies from Jupiter were manipulated through the Three Adepts and 40 Agents of the Great White Brotherhood, for the benefit of all mankind upon Earth and for all the terrestrial mental planes. This came during the great Configuration of Planets in 1962, when the potentially benign energies radiated by the Configuration would have been so mutated by the wrong thought and action of terrestrials as to be disasterous to them. More devastating catastrophies than the world can remember would have caused the death and destruction of tens of thousands of human lives had not this Emergency Power Transmission been given. Between January 30th and February 19th, 1962, 8 such very special Transmissions were given through the Three Adepts.

OPERATION WORLD HEALING, POWER TRANSMISSION:

On November 14th, 1963, a Basic Power Manipulation was given through the Three Adepts to help prevent the spread of a deadly disease wave then being generated in Asia, threatening the health and lives of millions of people throughout the world. Severe local interference was encountered from elements of the dark forces who were trying to prevent the success of Operation World Healing. While Two of the Three Adepts continued the Power Transmission, the Third was dispatched, with the help of a special Operator from another Planet, to put an end to this interference, in a dangerous and direct encounter with powerful forces of evil. This was one of the 12 Emergency Power Transmissions given through the Three Adepts between November 13th and December 26th, 1963.

NOVEMBER 1964–EMERGENCY POWER TRANSMISSION:

A combination Special and Basic Power Manipulation was held on November 19th, 1964, at the beginning of an Emergency Period upon Earth. In this Transmission, tremendous energies were radiated through the Three Adepts, the Great White Brotherhood and basic cooperators in order to help bring about necessary conditions for the evacuation of certain terrestrial Initiates from Earth, to undergo advanced Initiation. This emergency lasted until November 24th and 3 Special Power Transmissions were given through the Three Adepts.

EMERGENCY TRANSMISSION DURING THE SPECIAL MISSION:

A state of desperate emergency existed upon Earth on December 1st, 1965, when all available Spiritual Power Batteries of the Great White Brotherhood were charged by Mars Sector 6, in Satellite No.3. These Batteries had been depleted by the terrific energy demands of the Three Adepts, made while They were performing a Special Mission for the benefit of all mankind. One Battery proved defective under the great pressures being applied to it and had to be replaced. The Three Adepts requested a Power Transmission for terrestrial man, in spite of the fact that They had been specifically prohibited from helping mankind in this way for the duration of Their Special Mission. Nevertheless, in Their compassion for mankind, They made this request which was refused by Mars Sector 6.

OPERATION ONE ONE ONE, PRIOR TO JULY 8TH, 1964:

Prewarned of an impending emergency, the Three Adepts were standing by in Their Earth physical bodies on an immediate alert basis, on April 30th, 1961. The call came just before 10:00 p.m. and 120 SECONDS later They were all in deep Samadhic trance, radiating energy to the world. Minutes later They were all projected from Their bodies to locations of strategic importance; Adept Number One to the Andes in Peru, Adept Number Two to Mount Shasta and Adept Number Three to an undisclosed position over the Atlantic ocean. The Three Adepts formed a triangulation pattern and all mankind was heavily screened.

Then an Intelligence, known as Mars Sector 8, landed upon Earth and a Transmission of energy was begun to the very Logos of the Planet Herself, helping Her in Her self-imposed limitation and preparing Her for things yet to come. Prior to July 8th, 1964, there were 14 such Transmissions which were known by the code name "Operation One One One". Before and during each of these essential Transmissions of energy, the Three Adepts performed duties of vital importance.

OPERATION ONE ONE ONE, AFTER JULY 8TH, 1964:

A Special Power Manipulation on behalf of the Logos of Earth was given on November 22nd, 1966. In this Special Manipulation, the Master Aetherius, Himself, described the Transmission of Spiritual energy to the Goddess, Earth, through the Three Adepts and the two Gotha Agents—all under the direct supervision of the Supreme Masters of Saturn. This Transmission was held from 10:36 p.m. until 11:11 p.m. and was, to-date, the only performance of "Operation One One One" reported after July 8th, 1964.

THE COSMIC INITIATION OF EARTH, JULY 8TH, 1964:

"A momentous occasion in the history of the Solar System."

This is how the great Cosmic Master, Mars Sector 6, described the very Special Power Manipulation which He was directing on July 8th, 1964—a day now considered the Holiest of Holy Days by Members of The Aetherius Society throughout the world.

This Very Special Power Transmission began with two basic Phases through the Three Adepts. Then, following immediately, a Phase of "Operation One One One"—the familiar code name assigned to Transmissions of energy to the Logos of Earth—Herself. This was soon to prove unlike any previously reported Transmission, as a Solar Lord appeared to begin giving to Earth the greatest amount of energy She had ever received since Her last rebirth as a Planet. So great were the energies radiated by this Solar Lord, that there was, at one point, an Emergency Operation to keep Her from moving from Her orbit.

During this Cosmic Initiation of Earth, the Three Adepts projected from Their physical bodies and took up assigned positions. They were then enclosed within very tight etheric screens and terrific energy concentrations were then built up beneath these screens. Energy pressures reached unimaginable intensities under these conditions, but the Three Adepts held these pressures until the precisely correct time for their release. Then the process was repeated, again and again. There is no way to describe the incredible strain such an operation repeatedly put upon the etheric bodies of even such highly trained and evolved Beings as the Three Adepts, but They, nevertheless, survived this terrific ordeal in excellent condition. Their action during this Very Special Transmission was a vital and necessary part of this momentous occasion—the Cosmic Initiation of Earth.

The Cosmic Initiation of Earth took place between 10:00 p.m. and 10:54 p.m., Pacific daylight saving time, on July 8th, 1964—a fitting climax to, but by no means the end of the Spiritual Mission of the Three Adepts upon Earth. For as this inadequate record of Their sacrifice is being written, the Three Adepts are preparing to go into action again, this time in the most difficult and dangerous Mission They have ever faced upon this Planet. (Note 3.)

A study of even the briefest details of these difficult assignments will show any open-minded, thinking reader the high degree of specialization and the overall abilities of the Three Adepts. It should be noted that the tasks outlined above could not have been performed by other beings on Earth, not even the Great White Brotherhood, Who are highly specialized in certain essential facets of Metaphysical manipulation, but have not had the necessary lives of training in combat strategy that the Three Adepts have received in many different and varied theatres of operation. The Master Jesus was fully acquainted with these facts, hence His statement that these Three had proven to be the Saviours of a planetary race. As no individuals existed on Earth, in terrestrial bodies, with the same Karmic allowance as that endowed upon the Three Adepts during this time period, then no one else could have performed these particular assignments in the way that the Three Adepts performed them. This makes Them the Saviours of every man, woman, child, animal, fish, tree and rock upon the surface of this globe.

"You stood as little helpless children—by. Few of you even raised one hand in prayer, never mind your hearts, to help Those Who suffered for you. And yet, again and again and again and again, They stood and faced unbelievable odds on your behalf, for They cared for you. They loved you with a Love seldom shown by any other being to any other being."

In case some of you may feel that, because of the Interplanetary status of the Three Adepts, They were above pain, may I take the liberty of reminding you that these Three Beings operate in Earth physical bodies; that They are more sensitive to any stimuli than anyone else in a terrestrial body. During some of the Sorties mentioned, the Adepts received quite serious injuries. Although the Sorties took place when They were in a projected form, nevertheless, in most of them, They were in the equivalent of a terrestrial super-conscious body and not in "full aspect". Therefore, They could be and indeed were severely hurt many times during these bitter conflicts on the lower astral realms, against the fantastic odds which They had to meet. It must be remembered, too, that there is more energy on the lower astral realms than there is on even the Higher Realms. All thought forms projected by mankind, through his countless lives, are used by the black magicians, if they vibrate within a certain framework. As the mass thought of mankind throughout the centuries has been within this framework, the black magicians can therefore split these thought forms up and actually use the mental energy contained within them.

It is not by chance that the Three Adepts have been so active within a few years of the cessation of one of the greatest wars on the surface of this globe. The mass of thought and suffering, generated by human mentality during this conflict, settled on the plane upon which it could exist, namely the lower astral realms.

The black magicians knowing this, having engineered the war in the first place for just such a reason, were able to feed and, energetically speaking, "grow fat" upon these powerful and involved energies. That the Three Adepts could stand against such a vast energy potential is, in itself, one of the miracles of terrestrial time. They did so and They suffered very, very acute agony many times, knowing that if They failed, then terrestrial man would be but a pawn in the hands of superior, evil forces awaiting their opportunity to pounce in their power-mad struggle for supremacy.

The Master Jesus goes on to make the very statement that, had the Three Adepts not broken the bonds of slavery, you would—now—have been completely conquered by evil, the like of which none of you has ever come up against before, not even in your wildest imagination. (Note 7.)

"Seven times Blessed are the Three Adepts for Their greatness, for Their Love, for Their compassion, for the way that They have helped a planetary race to remain sane, for the way that They have broken the bonds of slavery which—make no doubt about it—would, by now, have bound you tight to your wicked masters.

"Seven times Blessed are each one of these mighty Beings for the way that They have, despite your disbelief, despite your scorn, despite your treatment of Them, They have rallied and stood as a barrier between the human race and the depths of hell's hell."

It appears from this statement by the Master Jesus, that there have been times throughout history when the Three Adepts, coming as They have done in one form or another throughout the centuries, have been very badly treated by terrestrial man. One of these Adepts, code named "Number Three", in one life, came as the biblical character "Samson". Although the history given in the Bible of "Samson" is incorrect and certainly incomplete, we are informed that it is a fact that He was actually blinded and He did die in the arena. He had a job to do on the physical plane of Earth and was instructed, by His Karmic Masters, to perform this assignment. Even though this Being did great good in this life, He nevertheless purposely fell into the trap laid for Him so that He could bring about the results dictated by His Cosmic assignment. What those results were is known only to the Karmic Lords and not to mankind, but undoubtedly essential results were brought about in the life He spent as "Samson" on Earth.

"Number Three" is not the only Adept Who has, before now, met disbelief, scorn and poor treatment, to say the least, at the hands of the very people He came to save from a fate very much worse than death.

There is no doubt that the human race on Earth, even today, is barbaric, especially with those who try to operate above the basic understanding of ignorant man. They demonstrate their ignorance in many different ways, but they will not be able to get away with this indefinitely for there are severe Karmic repercussions for bad treatment of a great Adept. People do not yet realize that the Karmic Law is absolutely just; that the Karmic Law acts very positively against any individual who performs any type of crime, be it large or small, against another individual who has dedicated his very life to such a tremendous task as the Three Adepts have chosen. If you punch the man next door on the nose, you will reap certain negative Karma. But were you even to speak in a disparaging way to One of the Adepts, whether you knew His identity consciously or not, your negative Karma would be several thousandfold of that caused by the assault on the man next door. Some people may think this statement is illogical. How, they may ask, could you be blamed for saying words against an Adept unless you knew His identity?

The point is, you do know this identity—but you have not allowed your super-consciousness to govern your basic consciousness.

Within all there is the Spark of God—the all-knowing Spark of God—that part which knows the identity of Beings such as the

Three Adepts, but few men have allowed this knowledge to permeate their conscious minds. Even some of those who have been exposed to the direct teachings of these Individuals, have not allowed themselves to admit the greatness of these Three Beings. Why? To do so would cause a complete change in their lives; complete in every way and few men are ready to make such a change. Therefore, the Law of Karma is not unjust, but, on the contrary, quite just in that the Karmic scales are tipped negatively against you for taking any action against such Beings as These.

Of course, on the positive side it is very different. The more you pray for such Beings, the more you WORK for Them, the more you help Them in every conceivable way possible to you, the greater is your Karmic reward.

Never forget, dear readers, that these Three Beings have saved you many times in the past from conditions worse than any belsen camp. Never, never forget that. If you have to forget all else, never forget that, for, if you do so now, there will come a time when your super-consciousness will remind you of it and your remorse will bring deep sorrow because then it may be too late for you to mend your ways.

"These are Blessed.
"These are Blessed in the minds of the greatest Masters in this System."

When Jesus states that These are Blessed by the greatest Minds in this System, He is, of course, referring to the Lords of the Sun. (Note 8.)

"These are Blessed in the minds of all good-thinking men, for if there be a man upon Earth who does not Bless These now— and yet knows of Their works—such a one as this has condemned himself to involution until his eyes be opened through painful experience."

On the mento-physical and mento-psychic levels there is very little known about the Three Adepts. But on the psycho-Spiritual levels much is known about Them. On the Higher Planes, inhabited by evolved beings who have lived upon this Earth and have passed on and await the correct time for their rebirth into the "physical" reincarnatory cycle, much time is spent in prayer and blessings for these Three mighty Beings. But upon the basic levels, as previously stated, man will not allow himself to see the trees even though he be in the midst of the forest. This sounds unbelievable, but is nevertheless true. Some people have been, in the past, exposed to certain of the exploits of these mighty Beings and yet they have turned away from Them. Such people, according to the Master Jesus—not according to the opinion of any earthman, but according to the knowledge of a great Cosmic Being—have caused involution to themselves until, as Jesus so aptly states: "...*his eyes be opened through painful experience."*

The Law is just and exact, for the mills of God grind slowly but they grind exceeding small. To use the statement of Jesus Himself, centuries ago: "As you sow so shall you reap." As you do unto others so shall they do unto you. If you treat one of the Adepts badly, He will not do the same unto you—if He did, you would not be sane today—but the Law, Itself, will cause those conditions to be brought into manifestation around you so that you might learn not to make the same mistake again and these lessons will be painful ones, if necessary.

"Blessed be the Three Adepts—now—for even again They stand between you and hell.

"It is, at this time, that those in the darker realms are waiting to spring their trap. For thousands of centuries they have planned this, carefully, move by move. Do you know man, not one single murderous dictator has been put into a position by chance? Conqueror after conqueror has been built up by the dark ones to act as a recruiting agent upon the physical plane of your world! These have brought around them like wickedness and have taken this

back to the lower realms with them, and have built the armies of evil there. It has been a plan cunningly conceived and you—the pawns in a game to gain a whole humanoid race. Did you know that man?

"I, Jesus, declare this to be, up till now, the secrets of secrets.

"Now they wait for their 'armageddon'. Their schemes are laid; their plots worked out; their strategy computed. They wait to move and you stand as a lamb would stand before a hungry lion, helpless, defenseless, wrapped up, involved by your own wrong thought and action, you stand—if you know—quaking.

"But between you and the others stand Three Glorious Lights.

"Three Lights—brilliant Lights, Lights of strength, Lights of power, Lights of knowledge and ability gained in the hardest schools of life."

The hells—foul, degrading, evil smelling, melting pot of all that is the very lowest dreggs of humanity. The melting pot of the most evil black magicians of Maldek, Lemuria, Atlantis and Kali Yuga. When you first go there, you will notice that it is a collection of cruel feudal systems; each coven ruled by the most powerful exponent in the black arts. You might conclude, after a first examination, that this is all there is to it—but you would be wrong—deadly wrong. Any interference with one of these covens and you feel, rather than see, vast minds behind them all. Minds which want it to appear as though these realms are split up, divided and will allow this appearance as long as the governing mind so declares. But if you really probe into the heart of the system there, you would find something which makes Dante's inferno as mild as a child's comic strip in comparison. You would be touched by the greater mind behind it all, the very soul of the lower realms itself! It would move, exploring every fibre of your physical and mental being with foul, contaminating mental hands. It would creep over you and through you and away from you, leaving you stripped naked, shaking out of sheer revulsion because you had been touched by those contaminating fingers, sadistic fingers; feeling, exploring mental tendrils which you would know could crush you in a moment.

You would be threatened; you would be attacked by gross thought forms, dripping, foul, evil-smelling substances upon you. And yet if you had the ability—and you would be rare if you did—to withstand such an onslaught, then the tactics would change as quickly as a lightning flash moves through the clouds. What had been evil, contaminating, utterly revolting, would change to a creeping, exploring, fawning thing. Your mind would be laid bare even as easily as a wharf man will lay a fish bare when he fillets it. The exploring tendrils would find the depths of your basic animalistic desires and these would be heaped in front of you, in a way far more lifelike and apparently far more real than any materialization upon the physical plane of Earth could ever be.

All the delights which you could desire in your most basic mind would be offered to you in such a way as to be individually appealing.

If you refused this—and if you had such an ability, you would be rare indeed—then would follow other promises, other materializations. You would be promised—and the promise proven to you— that you could enjoy immortality, power, or even insignificance.

You could be a ruler, or ruled, whichever you desired. You could spend your life in drugged illusion, or mental flights of fancy which would be specially designed to appeal to your mental outlook.

If all these things failed, then you would be attacked; battered from every source by vast, demolishing forces which would rise from the very pit of hell itself to tear you asunder, to consume your body, to consume your thoughts and your mind and revibrate them again onto a lower more usable level.

And the soul of you, stripped bare, would take many lives to overcome such terrible shock.

And in the last moment, before your soul was torn from your

body in the way that some savages have torn the heart from a human sacrifice, bleeding and warm, you would feel agony and mental anguish the like of which is hardly believable.

Then would your soul drift in shock, for many lives to come. This is the hell.

These, aye and even worse than these things—so terrible that I would not dare to publish them—face the mighty Three Lights as They go on Their main and last assignment on your behalf. It must be remembered, what makes it worse, these Beings, ultra-attuned and ultra-sensitive, are more revolted by conditions in the hells—which They know so well—than any earthman would be and yet They face them without hesitation.

They go, not for Themselves, but for a race which is alien to Them.

Not for Their relatives, not to save the world upon which They were born, but to save another world; a world which has, throughout the centuries, often turned against Them. They go to face this foulness, this terrible mental anguish, this indescribable contamination—They go even again. Neither will They look to the left nor the right until Their Mission is accomplished. Time and time again, dear readers, note—TIME AND TIME AGAIN—will these mighty Beings face terrible conditions and awful odds, and if They make one strategic error, Their Souls are put adrift to suffer the shock of absorption of the mind and body into the pit itself.

Do not think that the prominent black magicians sit, as would a witch doctor, in tiny hovels surrounded by weird symbols and grinning skulls, before a cauldron of bubbling, vile smelling substance. Some of them may do this, but certainly not the prominent ones. In fact, it is true to say that the more prominent the position held in the lower astral realms by a black magician, the more that magician is well-versed in modern technology—probably at least one to two centuries ahead of the technology of modern civilization known on the surface of this Planet.

Atomic chain reaction was discovered on the lower astral

realms years before it was discovered and used on the surface. In fact, the discoverers saw to it that it became a weapon in the hands of mankind.

The laser beam has been fully perfected in the lower astral realms and is a weapon capable of very accurate projection of a concentrated light beam over several miles. The internal temperatures of this laser beam, even at a range of five miles, are approximately triple that of the laser beam temperatures on Earth. The laser, perfected in the lower astrals, has been used as an offensive weapon for some time and even projectors, a little larger than a modern automatic pistol and weighing a little more but very useful and deadly in combat, are used regularly by almost all the black magicians and their henchmen.

They are also well-versed in all types of bacteriological offense and defense, especially the former. They can launch disease spores from a cannon in small capsules with deadly accuracy at ranges about the equivalent of 50 terrestrial miles. These capsules are fused to explode either on contact or at any time after contact as desired by those who launch them. The bacteria contained in these capsules is in a state of dormancy until released from the environmental conditions within the capsule. Then it becomes a minute but virulent and deadly killer. One of the most frequently used disease spores attacks through normal clothing, through the skin and into the spine causing a breakdown of the spinal fluid and eventually death. Another disease spore can enter through the skin causing coagulation of the blood, paralysis and death. Even another attacks the brain through the eyes, ears or strands of hair causing paralysis and death. Whole areas can be blanked off and saturated with these disease spores and, what is even worse, several different types of disease spores can be used in any one area at the same time, as there is a similarity in the environmental conditions necessary for their existence. Anyone attacked by these spores must not only prepare a defense—if possible—against one type of microbe, but also against other types as well. Although the essential environmental conditions of the disease microbes are somewhat similar, the defense against them is quite different. Therefore, three different types of disease spores, in capsules designed to explode at different time intervals, can be a strategic weapon and extremely difficult to combat.

The black magicians are also adept in the use of different forms of gas. The form most favored by them is the most deadly, as it is a radio-active gas, possibly a derivative of unstable isotopes. This gas can enter through any breathing passages, including the eyes and ears, or any exposed part of the skin and cause a very fast cellular breakup. A body, so attacked, becomes extremely radio-active and begins to disintegrate, causing the radio-activity to spread throughout a neighborhood. Defense against this radio-active gas is difficult as it is very quick acting. As soon as the reaction starts within a cellular structure, the cells affected speed up the reaction so that the whole process becomes cumulative from itself, as it were. This gas can be encapsulated, but, even worse, can be contained in rockets with atomic or hydrogen bomb warheads which can be controlled by highly sophisticated computer systems. When such a rocket explodes, not only is a thermo-nuclear explosion caused, but the saturation of a very wide area with powerful radio-active gas. As the gas is heavier than air, it will tend to sink *into* the ground, making the affected area far more radio-active than even a normal thermo-nuclear explosion would make it. Coupled to this, the gas is not consumed by the heat of the explosion, because the containers are specially designed to break away just prior to the main explosion so that the shock wave, produced by the chain reaction of the main explosion, disperses this highly radio-active gas over very wide areas. This is indeed an extremely deadly weapon, the overall effects of which are very difficult to combat.

The computer systems used by some of the most prominent black magicians are far in advance of anything now on Earth, as are the detector and guidance systems.

They also have robots, some of them life forms which have been "de-educated" by cruel brain-washing techniques so that they may be re-educated again to act quite fearlessly, as intelligent zombies, for their masters. The mechanical forms of robots, which have been perfected, are also very dangerous weapons, inasmuch as their reaction periods are far quicker, for the most part, than that of an intelligent life form. The robots carry powerful laser beams and various other energy projectors, all of which bring instantaneous death to an unprotected life form. The mechanical robots can enter spore fields and other contaminated areas to widen the area, because they can carry small spore and radioactive gas capsules and disperse these in a controlled manner. They are generally controlled by ultra-high frequency rays, or equivalent, emitted from sophisticated computers which can work out a pattern and guarantee the methodical contamination of every part of a chosen area.

They also have aircraft capable of higher velocities than anything on Earth, at the moment, and capable of carrying laser armament which is very deadly because, in conjunction with very sensitive detector beams operated by compact but highly efficient computer systems, the laser beams can be controlled so as to cover a wide area with fire power when the craft are flying in certain pre-arranged patterns. These craft are manned by controlled robots, life-form zombies, or even occasionally by the black magicians themselves, some of whom like the "sport" of the kill.

Their water craft are, for the most part, quite small, very fast and extremely manoeuverable. They are armed with atomic rockets, gas and spore containers, laser beams and other energy projectors which can be used against one another over considerable distances, but, for the most part, the water craft are used for local shore bombardment and assault.

Added to this type of armament are the protective barriers which the black magicians have perfected over the centuries. All their apparatus, even including hydrogen bombs, can be protected by force screens which form magnetic barriers around the projectile, or craft, or even the black magician himself and can be held in place by the radiation of power from computers and other sources. Some of these magnetic barriers could easily withstand a combined attack by heavy gunfire and aircraft from the largest aircraft carrier on Earth for weeks or even months, if necessary.

The most prominent of the black magicians, although rare, are also adept in the invocation of Devic forces which they can control and guide by their minds. This too is a very difficult procedure to defend oneself against, especially as—in the case of the Three Adepts—They cannot stoop to the same level in defense as the black magicians will in attack. Therefore, They have to adopt different procedures entirely when dealing with invoked and controlled basic Devic forces.

The black magicians are also expert in the formation of devastating thought forms which can be contaminated in any way they so desire.

All prominent black magicians in the lower hells can levitate and fly quickly through the air from one place to another. Some can de-materialize and re-materialize again, either in their normal shape, or even take on other forms which may better serve their nefarious purposes.

The most prominent ones have a high degree of psychic development and can read the thoughts of others very quickly and, in rare cases, actually interfere with and change another's thought pattern, sometimes over considerable distances.

This is a long way from the witch doctor sitting in his little hut surrounded by skulls, bats and toads, is it not? This should give you a little idea of some of the weaponry which will be used against the Three Adepts when They obey the Commandment, given to Them by the great Lords Who foresaw the rise of the evil forces against all terrestrial planes of existence.

When you take into consideration that Beings of sensitivity, Spirituality and glorious Light face such fantastic odds and "advanced" weaponry as that described, you must also realize that Their actions are strictly limited, for They cannot stoop to the depths which Their adversary will not hesitate to adopt. They must act strictly within the confines of the Karmic Law with understanding and, above all, compassionate mercy for those intent upon causing Them a fate far worse than any death upon the physical realm. This is how it will be and it will go on being like that over and over again—until the battle is over!

When the Three Adepts, helped by Two more specially trained Beings of Interplanetary Stature, fought the alien in the lower astral realms, this battle itself lasted through 27 Sorties. (Note 4.) In the correct time sequence, each of these Sorties lasted at least several hours, if not days—probably some of them even weeks. For it must be remembered that in travel from one physical realm to another plane of existence one enters into a different time sequence. What happens on your realm in one hour, might take several hours to happen upon another plane of existence. This is a fact, whether one projects to the other side of the Universe or to another mental plane. Time is relative from the point of reference only.

The Three Adepts living among you, eating the same food, wearing the same clothes—wherever They may be—during Their next Mission to save you from total slavery imposed by the minds who built the hitlers and the himmlers throughout history, will be burning the midnight oil while you sleep in blissful ignorance. And as They burn it, They will know that, even were They to awake the majority, They would be treated with disbelief and scorn—yet They will go on and on throughout the coming months.

Unlike the average earthman who accepts responsibilities in relation to the monetary fee he receives, these Great Beings have NOT given mankind a bill which must be paid, or promised before Their assignment starts. If an actress is worth hundreds of thousands of dollars to act a part in an unimportant film, what are the Three worth to save a whole planetary race? It would not be easy to compute Their worth by Earth standards. Even so They have

NOT made any materialistic demands on any man for what They are about to do for humanity.

Theirs is the height of true Spirituality. Indeed was the Master right when He said: "By their works shall ye know them." Not by Their appearance, not by Their theory, not because They sit cross-legged in isolation and in bliss—not caring for the plight of humanity—but by Their WORKS; Their works not even on Their own Planet; Their works in the hell of the lowest Planet in this Solar System---!

Try to imagine, if you can, the vast responsibilities which must lie upon the shoulders of these Three Adepts.

They know that if They die and the vast energy of Their mentalities be absorbed into the devils in the hells, mankind will perish, for he will not know how to begin to fight this concentrated evil—never mind defeat it!

Therefore, with every move They make, They take the risk of not only condemning Themselves, but each and everyone of you.

They know that if Their strategy is broken and Their protective barriers forced down by overwhelming odds, every little child upon Earth will become the victim of a devil's foulness.

There is not one person reading this who can in all honesty say that they would be willing to take the responsibility of making decisions which could have an outcome of such vast importance as this.

Now is there---?

And yet, as much as the Three Adepts Themselves must loath and be revolted by the very idea of coming into conflict with such great odds—especially when the outcome is not only Their own destruction, but the destruction of every man, woman and child on a whole Planet—They will not falter. A realization of this will give you some little idea of the vast responsibilities which lie upon the shoulders of these Three shining Lights.

Good Members of The Aetherius Society have, since their first exposure to some of the feats of the Three Adepts, stated in all honesty that they did not feel worthy of such intervention by such Beings. Many have stated that they could not see WHY such Beings as these should suffer so much upon their behalf. The answer to the latter part of the statement can be given in four simple words with a meaning which reaches to the far ends of space—TRUE Love in action.

"*Three Lights of Service.*

"*Three Lights of God. Yes, Three Lights of God bearing the swords of Karma, protected by the armour of Their complete Spiritual dedication to God's Cause.*

"*Blessed are the Three Adepts.*"

Were it not for the complete and absolute dedication to Their cause, the Three Adepts could never stand against such overwhelming odds as those which They will meet, over and over again, during Their next Mission for the salvation of mankind. They have been specially trained in many different theatres of operation to withstand great odds and stupendous antagonistic pressures, keeping always the predetermined Spiritual goal in view. No matter how hard the way to this goal, They keep it plainly in sight. It is as a guiding light from the Lords Themselves which beckons Them onward, which inspires Them, which gives to Them super-human strength, super-normal mental abilities which enabled Them in the past—and we pray God will enable Them in the future—to press on towards Their predetermined goal.

Oh my God, what could we do without the Three Adepts?

We should all thank God for allowing the Three Adepts to be upon Earth, at this time, to save us from the worst of the very worst.

But for Them, we would be crushed in one mighty stroke.

We would be powerless.

We would be sniveling, insane slaves in the hands of such sadistic evil as that which exists in the pit of hell itself.

Indeed, aye indeed, it is the justice of the Law, woe unto

EVERY man who should turn away from Beings Who have pledged to do so much for so many.

"THESE THREE HAVE DONE MORE FOR THE HUMAN RACE THAN ANY OTHER THREE MASTERS WHO HAVE EVER CONTACTED THE HUMAN RACE AT ANY TIME UPON THIS PLANET.

"*In comparison with what They have done for you, my task and the results of what I did were naught, were not even worthy of mention! I, Jesus, whom you murdered and who rose again to prove to you a great Spiritual Truth, have made this declaration before my God!*"

This statement was made on oath by the Master Jesus Himself.

The same Jesus Who came to Earth in order to perform two missions. The first, to die. The second in importance, to give teaching to a backward race in order to bring to them the realization of oneness with God.

He died, and died horribly—so that a catastrophe due to ravage the human race could be avoided because He took upon Himself the Karma of the race and thereby avoided this terrible calamity, so that man might gain further experience in this classroom called Earth. Naturally, this Karma has to be balanced by each and every lifestream upon Earth at sometime or another. I personally feel that those people who are dedicated in active service for humanity are a few of those who benefited, Karmically, by the death of Jesus and are now paying back their Karmic debt by their dedication. Those who have not yet started to pay back this debt will, sooner or later, have to do so; no doubt with interest which has accumulated throughout the centuries. Because these were late in starting, they must have accumulated even more negative Karma against themselves.

Even as a young man I had this Truth presented to me in a vision. I knew that we owed the Master Jesus much and I knew that the only way for mankind to pay this debt was to devote himself to education, healing and service to humanity. It was in those days, now many years ago, that I made up my mind to do just this. I feel that many people have had, if not a vision of this nature, then an inner feeling that they should do the same and so great has been their conviction, that these people have virtually dedicated themselves in service towards this great end.

The teachings of Jesus were, in every way, superb.

They were not new because, some five centuries before Jesus, the Lord Buddha had given very similar teachings to another part of the world. But Jesus came and mixed more with the multitudes than did Buddha. His teachings were far more simply given than were Buddha's and, probably because of this, less understood. It is simplicity which is not understood in this world. Nevertheless, He came with a way of life and those who have followed this way of life throughout the centuries, have now dedicated themselves in service to humanity.

To give you one example, every Member of The Aetherius Society—except one—was alive on this Earth in the time of Jesus. Many of these Members have now realized this in one way or another. Some of them—unfortunately not all—have dedicated their life, in different degrees, to The Aetherius Society because they realize that it is through the Society that the great Cosmic Teachings are given. So therefore, naturally, it is the Society which will be used in the future by the great Masters to bring about Their visualized conditions on this Earth. (Note 9.)

Naturally, this is not the only organization working for the benefit of mankind. But it is certainly one of the most essential according to the words of the Cosmic Masters Themselves.(Note 9.)

Even though the great Master Jesus saved a horrible catastrophe befalling mankind, even though He gave to mankind a superior way of life towards peace and Spiritual harmony, He nevertheless states in this Blessing, quite definitely in so many words, that:

"In comparison with what They have done for you, my task

and the results of what I did were naught, were not even worthy of mention!"

This statement stands by itself, stands as Truth and will stand, despite all disbelief, as an aspect of lasting Truth in the Akashic Records of this Earth.

This should give you some little idea of the great tasks which the Three Adepts have already done for you, not to mention that which They are about to do.

Stop reading now and put up your arms, palms extended outwards, close your eyes and thank God for these Beings. This is the least you can do in the light of what Jesus Himself has told you.

Do not forget that Jesus commands you to do this.

"This is Truth!
"Indeed, indeed Blessed are These Ones.
"They should always be Blessed by each and everyone of you. Never should a day pass but what you Bless These. You should devote your whole life in Service to These, for by serving Them, you serve all men—and even vastly more important than this—you serve the Karmic Gods."

You have already read the declaration by the Ascended Master of the Great White Brotherhood, Saint Goo-Ling, Who has made it quite plain to all, the dire necessity for Spiritual man now to rise into action. You have also read the magnificent Transmission by the Master Jesus—Himself, Who has told you WHY you should rise in these days. You have read and studied the commentary on both of these magnificent Messages and in that commentary you have learned why Saint Goo-Ling and the Master Jesus chose this strategic time to release Their Power to the Three Adepts, and also to prepare men of good heart by making these declarations. You have read and by now should have some small idea of the hells and even what the next Mission of the Three Adepts, on your behalf, may be like. Now, in the last quotation from the Transmission, you have been given definite instructions by Jesus Himself. If you obey these instructions, you can play your part and so help the Powers of Light to be successful. By doing this, you will be helping mankind in its darkest hour---!

When I first started to write the commentary on this Transmission, I intended to be as brief as possible so that this book could be prepared quickly and the essence of its Truth could be studied by Members and sympathizers of The Aetherius Society and all Metaphysical students, as soon as possible after it was originally given. However, there is always more in a Transmission than meets the eye. As I continued to go deeper into it, I realized that it was my duty, as a teacher, to deal with it far more fully than I originally intended. I think that you will agree that, in the commentary, this has been done at least to the best of my ability.

My original intention, before I started to write, was to deal very briefly, indeed, with the last passage quoted. However, again, it would not be doing the Transmission or the readers justice if I did not make it very plain to all of you what the Master Jesus means in this vitally important passage. So therefore, I feel that this should be dealt with at some length, and all the people who are destined to read this book, put in different categories so that they may all be educated HOW TO OBEY this latest Commandment given by the great Master.

In view of the specialized content of this Transmission, given when it was for the reason that it was, I give below some brief suggestions as to what different categories of people should do about this, in the light of the last Commandment by Jesus Himself.

CATEGORY 1: Those who are not familiar with The Aetherius Society teachings.

If you are unfamiliar with The Aetherius Society teachings, then you can still obey this Commandment without it interferring in the least with any religious belief or calling you may have chosen.

You should read the books recommended herein, because they will give you a deeper understanding of your evolutionary paths and, in the case of "The Twelve Blessings", give you some definite Spiritual exercises and prayers which you can practise regularly and thereby enhance your appreciation and awareness of all Sacred things. As well as this, of course, you can practise the prayer given by Jesus at the end of His wonderful speech. To practise this or any other prayer in "The Twelve Blessings" correctly, you should follow a very basic hygienic ritual. First of all, bathe so that the body is scrupulously clean.

Next, put on clean dress, whatever you may choose, but not one that you normally wear for every day work. In fact, if you can put aside special prayer clothes, you should do so.

Then you should prepare your room accordingly, if this is possible. The room should be, of course, clean; incense should be burning—I recommend the delicate Indian type of incense rather than the pungent type. The room should be slightly darkened, but should not be black dark. For the best results, the room should be prepared about 15 minutes before you start your prayer or, if you wish, while you are bathing or dressing for the practice. If you like the idea of colour—and all Metaphysical students should do because colour is helpful in all aspects of our daily lives—you should use a green bulb, this being the colour of balance because of its mid-spectrum position. Then stand and face the East, and put out your arms with palms facing outwards. Make sure that the body is relaxed and there is no tension in the neck or shoulders as forces cannot flow easily through tense muscles and nerves. Then you should say the whole prayer, as given by Jesus on this occasion, with as much of your heart as possible. This does not mean that you shout it to the house tops—certainly not—but you should try to say this prayer as though you really meant every word of it, putting all of your heart and especially your love into it.

The minimum that you should perform this prayer is once per day; more times if possible.

Please note that, although you may consider the power you release to be insignificant, if enough people said this prayer, following the suggestions given, then such a tremendous power of love would be radiated as to help greatly the Three Adepts in Their terrible struggles. Do not ever think that you will be doing this alone, or that you should not bother to do it because of your insignificance. Both thoughts are wrong and you would not be obeying the vital Commandment given by the Master Jesus.

CATEGORY 2: Sympathizers who are unable to attend classes, lectures, Divine Services and power circles at a Branch or Headquarters.

There are many people already in this category who cannot attend Headquarters or Branches, because of the distance they live away from Headquarters or Branches; in many cases because they live in other countries. Many of these have, in the past, bought our literature and have read it. Some of them have even written letters with questions about it. You should turn again to "The Nine Freedoms", "The Day The Gods Came" and "The Twelve Blessings", studying the first two of these very carefully and practising the prayers in the Blessings as much as possible. You, too, should adopt the suggestions given to Category 1 and say the prayer given by the Master Jesus at the *minimum* of three times a day.

Another valuable suggestion to you people would be to order The Aetherius Society Newsletter, because announcements of special prayer and power circles will be given. It is obvious that the Society will be extremely active during this next Mission and, when possible, a whole programme of prayer times will be announced in our Newsletter. So make sure that you are on the mailing list and receiving this information, so that you may join in at these significant times with all the rest of the people who will be praying at that time throughout the world. This, of course, will greatly enhance the good that you will do and the help that you will give, and make your obedience to the Commandment of Jesus many hundreds of times more potent than it would be normally.

CATEGORY 3: Sympathizers who are able to attend classes, lectures, Divine Services and power circles at a Branch or Headquarters.

You are fortunate inasmuch as you can come to our Services, lectures, classes and Divine Services, and you should never miss an opportunity to do so—*especially in the months to come*. Whenever you attend a Service given by the Society, you join together with others of similar Spiritual aspirations and the culmination of your efforts is a much stronger power release, per head, than you can normally invoke by practising alone—without guidance—on your own premises. This is not the opinion of any terrestrial, but an Occult Truth revealed by the Masters many times in the past. Coupled with this, of course, you are able to tune in, under direction at our Headquarters, to the tremendous radiations coming from Satellite No.3 to all Spiritual men upon Earth. (Note 2.) When you do this, you enhance your potential some 3000 times. Therefore, you can become a tremendous power for good and also obey the important Commandment, given by the Master Jesus, in a very potent manner.

You should say the new prayer of Jesus, printed herein, *at least* three times per day, adopting the procedure given to Category 1 in regard to room and personal preparation.

This is little to give in return for what the Three Adepts will be doing for you as soon as Their Mission starts and thereafter.

You, too, should avidly study the Newsletter so that you will be fully informed of special power circles, prayer circles and classes which will be arranged throughout the world by The Aetherius Society during this next Mission. Whenever humanly possible, you should attend these functions so that you can be directed, in a balanced way, to send out your power with others to help the Forces of Light in Their battle for you. Please remember that the majority of these special Services will be open to Members and non-members alike. You do not have to become a Member of The Aetherius Society in order to come along and thus obey the Commandment of Jesus in your most potent way. Read and carefully study all the textbooks recommended herein so that your awareness may be deepened. This will greatly improve your abilities and enhance the potency of all your prayers on behalf of the Three Adepts.

CATEGORY 4: Members who are unable to attend Divine Services, classes, lectures and power circles at a Branch or Headquarters.

There are many Members who, because of distance, are unable to attend our Special Services and will be unable to attend during the coming Mission. It is assumed, of course, that you all take our Newsletter, therefore you will be familiar with it and will be informed through it when special prayer sessions, power circles and classes will be held at the Headquarters for and on behalf of the Three Adepts. When you receive such information, you should make your preparations and tune in at the same time, if at all possible, that the Services are being held. You should practise "The Twelve Blessings" and practise the prayer, given by the Master Jesus in this Transmission, in the way already recommended, at the very minimum of *five times a day*. You should read the word of the Cosmic Masters as published by your Society, for every time you read these Transmissions, you are put in tune with the Higher Forces.

You might also like to adopt this suggestion; it is sometimes a quick way to get above your everyday work life by taking one of the Transmissions already published, and read a part of it out loud. Members who have tried this have experienced the great upliftment and thrill of the wisdom given in these magnificent speeches. I think that, if you try this, you can often put yourself in tune very quickly. This is especially true with "The Twelve Blessings". If you sit alone in a room, or even with your family if they wish to hear you read, and read out one of "The Twelve Blessings", you will find that you will feel quite different after it than before you started—and this can be a quick way to overcome the depressions and limitations of a work-a-day world. You should also adopt the suggestions given to the previous categories regarding reading the Society literature as this is, for the most part, the WORD of the Cosmic Masters. You should also try to *plan your vacations* so that you can attend the Headquarters in London or Los Angeles during them. If this is not possible, then arrange vacations so that you can attend Branch activities.

These are the ways in which you can obey the latest Commandment given by Jesus and help the Powers of Light in Their desperate struggle to save YOU from the merciless devils from hell itself.

CATEGORY 5: Members who are able to attend all Services, lectures and other activities at a Branch or at a Headquarters.

You are in the fortunate position of living near enough to a Branch or Headquarters to be able to attend all or certainly most of our activities—and you should do so. Especially in the light of this Transmission from the Master Jesus and the fact that these are indeed the darkest hours for mankind, *you should consider this your absolute duty to do so*. Never should you miss any activity if it can possibly be avoided.

You people could be the very backbone of terrestrial help to the Three Adepts during this time.

And if you fail in this duty, then you cannot help but set yourself back. The Master Saint Goo-Ling, in His Transmission, made this very plain because it was obviously His motive to give advice which would be the most helpful to people in these days. You are in the fortunate position of being able to help in a very potent manner—and you most certainly should never miss an opportunity to do so.

Naturally you, too, should study the Newsletter for special announcements. You will often receive special announcements, which cannot be printed in the Newsletter, of special activities which will be held during this next Mission of the Three Adepts, and you should be prepared to drop *everything* to attend these activities, no matter what or when they are. For it should be remembered that even a class or lecture held at the Headquarters and Branches of the Society can put you in tune, while you are actually listening, with a greater aspect of The Aetherius Society which exists on the Higher Mental Realms.

Yes, it is an absolute fact that the Society has more Members on the Higher Mental Realms, by far, than it does on the physical plane of Earth.

While you are "contained" within our atmosphere, you are not only learning, so that you can advance quicker than in ANY other way, but also you become a cell in the body of the overall Soul of the Society of the Masters and you are "touched" by the minds of that part of the organization which is in the Higher Mental Realms, who will be tuning in at the same time that activities are being conducted on this plane—receiving their instructions and teachings even as you are receiving yours. Therefore, attendance is, if used correctly and this fully realized, a great Spiritual experience in itself, no matter what activity you attend. Even if it only be a mundane business meeting, which I am very glad to say are very far and few between as far as Members are concerned, you will still be "touched" by the most evolved part of this Society.

You should say this new prayer of Jesus at the minimum of seven or nine times a day—more if possible. You should adopt the procedure of room and personal preparation recommended to Category 1 before you say this prayer.

Some Members, living near enough either to the London or Los Angeles Headquarters, have already volunteered to be on call for 24 hours a day for work teams, prayer circles and power circles during the coming emergency. ALL Members who can possibly volunteer for such essential duty should do so at once, especially in the light of the next Mission which will need the help of all of you. As most of you have to work during the daytime and are unable to be on call, then you should volunteer to be on call during those times when you are available—evenings, weekends and the like.

CATEGORY 6: Staff Members, Committee and Directors.

This is not the place to give you your instructions for they could be strictly classified, but you can guarantee that your actions will be counted upon many times during this next Mission. Special instructions will be issued in the appropriate manner.

If you belong to any of the above-mentioned categories, you can help in this Mission and thus obey the Commandment of the Master Jesus and those given by Saint Goo-Ling.

Never forget, please, that Saint Goo-Ling stated: *"Be ye prepared to work for right—for this is the hour! The hour of the prophecies. The hour of the turning point of evolution, or the hour of the defeat of all which is good and Holy upon Earth."*

In the light of this statement, all good men will want to expend as much effort and energy as possible to bring about those conditions which will not only save that which is good and Holy, but give it such a firm root upon this Planet that never again can it be threatened in the way that it is now being threatened. If the Three Adepts are successful in Their Mission, then gradually will a Spiritual awakening come to mankind. An awakening which, up to now, has only been allowed to grow so high and so strong before it has been choked by forces which are afraid of it. The Three Adepts will try, with Their lives if necessary, to bring about those conditions which will allow a new plant of Spirituality to be placed in the Soul of man, which will survive all the rigors of the future. This, dear readers, is what you will be working for by obeying the Commandment of Jesus and the advice given herein. There is no greater project on Earth today to which you can turn your hand, your heart and your mind---is there?

"*At this time may the great Spiritual Flame of protection surround These Three.*
"*I Bless Them with all my heart, with all my Soul.*
"*I BLESS THEM WITH ALL MY SPIRIT.*

(Jesus intoned a mystical Mantra of Power Invocation.)

"*I now invoke a Power for and on behalf of the Three Lights.*

(A further intoning of a mystical Power Mantra followed.)

"*Blessed are the Three Adepts for what They are about to do.*
"*So endeth this Blessing.*
"*Oh adorable children, be strong at this time. Reach upwards and inwards to the Light which shineth there, then come outwards dedicated in Spiritual Service to all and you will never regret this step.*
"*Oh Divine and Wondrous Spirit,*
Oh Everlasting Lord of Supreme Hosts,
We pray, at this time, that Your unquenchable Light,
That the Power of Your compassion illuminates and protects
The Three Adepts in Their greatest trial.
Oh Divine and Wondrous God,
May They succeed in Their Mission.
May They save helpless humanity from the monsters,
Which it has created.
Oh Mighty God,
Give us all the strength to stand, unflinchingly,
By the side of These,
So that a Spiritual Triumph might be born upon Earth.

Oh Divine Father of all Wondrous Creation,
We raise our minds to You—now,
Requesting that Your Power may fall upon the heads,
And penetrate the hearts of all men.

*So that they may be stronger in their Spiritual purpose.
So that they may live and act in the Light of God knowledge,
Forever and forever.*

"*I* came, at this time, to Bless the Three and to tell you all of these things.

"*May you be guided by your Spirit.*

"*Oh little children, become fully grown by acting upon these things, then will you: go with God.*"

Wonderful words by a truly great, compassionate Master of Love—Jesus.

Both of these Transmissions are definite, straight-to-the-point revelations of the most potent Truths in these days and they carry with them a glorious and magnificent promise for the future of mankind, if only he will allow that spark of greatness within him to guide the actions of his materialistic mind and body.

For thousands of years, man has gone about his everyday life in ignorance of the movement of titanic forces around him. Throughout the centuries, he has sprung from the bud into the leaf and been blown from the tree, in the autumn of his life, to pass to another plane of existence and again return as a bud to the tree of reincarnation. Few men have ever looked past the little branch, on which they grew, to see the great world beneath them. They have become wrapped up and involved to such an extent that even their psychic vision is dulled into unrecognizable dormancy. It is because this is so that Beings, like the great Lord of Compassion—Jesus, had to come at this time with this warning for mankind. Had the vision of man been unimpaired, as it should have been, he would have been able to conclude for himself that the time of the "armageddon" was close. For it is an obvious thing that, after the release of titanic energies to this Earth during Her Cosmic Initiation in July 1964, the powers of darkness would begin to see the writing on the wall. Would begin to feel that unless they moved, and moved decisively and quickly, they would be transmuted from the position which they had held onto so fervently, in some cases, for centuries and this transmutation would put them onto a different level of existence to be born again on the reincarnatory tree, suffering gross limitation.

To refer back to the Transmission by Jesus, He states that the great Hierarchal Lords could foresee these events for They obviously, even in those distant days, could see the exact time of the Initiation of Earth. They could also plainly see, with Their unimpaired Spiritual abilities, that the demons of darkness in the lower hells would see, from this Initiation, the beginning of their end. The Great Ones brought the Three Adepts to Earth in anticipation of the Initiation of Earth and, most definitely, in the full light of the knowledge of the rising up, by the evil ones, after this stupendous Cosmic event. (Note 3.)

Since the Initiation of Earth, all vibrations of all matter upon Earth are gradually quickening. There is a great natural speeding up of all life and all environmental conditions on this Planet. Even the ultra-violet emanations from the Sun are more potent today than they were prior to July 1964. You do not have to be a scientist to know this, you just have to work outside in the sunlight for a couple of days to prove this for yourself. It is this quickening which has caused the forces of darkness to make ready for their next major moves, namely that of the enslavement of all life forms upon the surface of this globe. It is in anticipation of just such a move, that the Three Adepts are here, with you, at this time. It is to inform you of these facts that the great Master Jesus Himself gave the Transmission you have just had the privilege of reading. It is to remind you that tomorrow is not just another day in your life, but a vital day nearer the decisive battle between the greatest good and basest evil on this Planet.

Even centuries ago, the mythologies of various creeds spoke about the coming of such a time as this. But only the Great Ones knew the hour when the uprising would start.

Jesus Himself has now made available, to all men destined to read His word, the truth of this hour. He has made His appeal.

It is now up to all men of Spiritual integrity to answer the appeal made by Jesus for help and assistance to the Three Adepts, at this—the most decisive time in the history of man upon Earth.

AUTHOR'S RECOMMENDATIONS

Note 1. See *The Nine Freedoms* (pages 109-137) for an eye-witness description of the Initiation of Ascension—one of the few ever reported in book form.

Note 2. Read *The Nine Freedoms* (pages 85-92) for a detailed description of the Third Satellite and a Magnetization Period. All dates of these Holy Periods are published, in advance, in *The Aetherius Society Newsletter* available to all on subscription.

Note 3. Read *The Day The Gods Came* for the ONLY published record in the world, giving FULL details of the great Cosmic event—the Initiation of Earth.

Note 4. See, also, *The Five Temples Of God* for further information regarding the Three Adepts. Also read *The Aetherius Society Newsletter* Volume 4, Issues 16, 17, 18, 19, 20, 21, 22, 23 and 24 for further detailed accounts of action taken by the Three Adepts on behalf of mankind.

Note 5. This refers to *The Five Temples Of God*, a Transmission delivered by the Master Aetherius on August 26th, 1967.

Note 6. See *The Nine Freedoms* for details of the evolution possible to all sentient beings in this Solar System.

Note 7. See *The Aetherius Society Newsletter* Volume 4, Issues 16, 17, 18, 19, 20, 21, 22, 23 and 24 for accounts of the attempted invasion of the physical planes of Earth from the hells, by a powerful android which had been in suspended animation for centuries until activated to move against mankind by its evil, extra-galactic controllers.

Note 8. See *The Nine Freedoms* for a deeper appreciation of the true greatness and majesty of the Lords of the Sun.

Note 9. Read *The Five Temples Of God* for an outline of the major assignments given by the Cosmic Masters to The Aetherius Society for the next 1000 years!

All above recommended books are obtainable from the Publishers of *The Three Saviours Are Here!*

CHAPTER FOUR

"OPERATION KARMALIGHT"

A little over a month after the delivery of the two Transmissions described in this book, the great battle between the Power of Light and the forces of darkness — officially called "Operation Karmalight" — began in deadly earnest. Acting under the highest Karmic Authority and permission, The Three Adepts entered the lower astral Realms of Earth on October 26th, 1967, at 21:11 hours, to perform Phase 1 of a Mission which was vitally important to every living entity on this Planet. The Three Adepts were joined by Their other Two Comrades and came up against stupendous odds during Phase 1. After an engagement with the denizens of the lower astral Realms lasting — in our time-frame sequence — 61 minutes, 5 seconds, The Five Adepts retreated to devise Their strategy.

During this Mission the author, chosen by the Cosmic Masters Themselves to be the only Mental Channel on Earth through whom "Operation Karmalight" was reported, went into a self-precipitated, deep Samadhic trance so that the Cosmic Master Aetherius could describe all but three Phases of "Operation Karmalight" in vivid detail.

Three recordings were made on professional tape recorders of each of these Phases. As it was the responsibility of The Aetherius Society to protect these reports, unique in the history of the world, each complete series of tape recordings were stored in three different places in the world. Later, when the Mission was over, the tape recordings were brought out of their respective vaults, carefully examined, re-spooled, re-labelled and carefully packed by a team of devoted Staff Team Members into sealed, non-magnetic, film shipping containers of great strength and each of the tapes was then carefully logged and stored again in vaults under special conditions. The expense of this procedure was quite considerable, but it must be remembered that the tapes recorded during "Operation Karmalight" were unique in philosophical history; therefore, it was our responsibility to preserve them in the best way possible for future generations.

Every Transmission delivered by The Master Aetherius through Doctor George King regarding the action of The Five Adepts, both in the hells and on the Higher Planes, was treated in the same manner.

"Operation Karmalight" proved to be an extremely difficult and very dangerous Mission indeed for The Five Adepts. By Karmic Law it had to end in a predetermined way and what made matters far more difficult, there was a time limit set upon the completion of the Mission. The main reason for "Operation Karmalight" was to seek out and transmute that entity — who had ruled the hells for countless centuries — known as satan. Satan, possessing knowledge and cunning, did not rule on a throne like a dictator, but carefully wrapped his identity up in four different physical forms and scores of different identities, and although his word in the hells was law which had to be obeyed on pain of a cruel death, he nevertheless was able to protect himself by the cunning concealment of his true form which took the shape of a male or female as and when he so desired. It must be remembered that The Adepts were working under stupendous limitations, imposed by the Karmic pattern of the human race, and this made the titanic conflict so much more difficult for Them.

The last Phase had to be arranged so that The Master Babaji, Spiritual and Political Leader of The Spiritual Hierarchy Of Earth, was brought into a man-to-man conflict with the last surviving aspect of the evil monster, satan.

This was dictated by Karmic Law and The Adepts and The Lord Babaji obeyed the Law strictly to the letter.

Those of you who have never been engaged in this type of conflict of military might and magic will have no real conception of its horrors and its apparently insurmountable difficulties. Remember, and never forget this, that there were, for the most part, only Five and occasionally Six Entities working under strict limitations, pitted against the mighty armies of the deadliest fighters in the world, those in the hells.

Never has there been a battle fought for mankind quite like this and we all should pray to God that never again will it be necessary.

During every one of the 24 Phases of "Operation Karmalight," The Adepts used Their magical skills and military prowess in a very humane way. In fact, They displayed a degree of humanity towards Their antagonist not demonstrated by any Earth men.

The 24 Phases of "Operation Karmalight" were conducted strictly — but strictly — in accordance with Karmic Law. During the last Phase, in answer to the demand of the Karmic Law, The Lord Babaji Himself came into mortal combat with the last surviving aspect of the most cunning, most clever and most versed evil magician upon Earth, and you should thank your God that The Lord Babaji won this conflict and caused a transmutation of this last aspect of satan. This happened during Phase 24, enacted on February 24th, 1969, between 21:50 and 22:47 hours Pacific Standard Time.

The other bodies or aspects of satan had been detected and transmuted one by one by The Adepts before this last conflict began. When The Lord Babaji, acting as The Sixth Adept, transmuted the fourth and last aspect of the ruler of the hells, this brought "Operation Karmalight" to an end. The Mission had been successfully accomplished, in that the most powerful evil magician on the Planet Earth had been transmuted and his consciousness broken up into over 1,000 different parts, so that each part would — by the Law of Karma — be introduced into the reincarnatory cycle of rebirth under strict limitations dictated by this same Law.

"Operation Karmalight," starting on October 26th, 1967, at 21:11 hours, and ending on February 24th, 1969, at 22:47 hours, lasted for 16 months.

Life on The Aetherius Society Staff, especially in the American Headquarters, during this time was one of constant readiness, constant self-protection from interfering forces, coupled with traumatic experiences the like of which few of you have ever experienced. At any time of the day or night, Doctor George King would be informed of the next Transmission and would, although physically and mentally tired, as well as at times being really ill — as he was injured more than once during the times he took these Transmissions — he still, without any hesitation or thought for his own welfare, took his place behind the three microphones in the tiny Transmission Room at the Headquarters.

The Adepts deserve all your Prayers and all your praise: so does Doctor King who suffered very much as Primary Terrestrial Mental Channel through whom the brilliant descriptions by The Master Aetherius were given so that they could be preserved for posterity.

During "Operation Karmalight" Doctor George King was in trance for a total of 24 hours, 12 minutes, 35 seconds, in the time-frame sequence of the physical Realms of this Planet. Exactly what this meant in the time-frame sequence of the lower astral Realms we do not know, but you should all be made aware that the average time he was in trance during each of the 24 Phases was 1 hour and 31 seconds! Even if these had been message Transmissions, as were the two you have read in this book, never mind Transmissions describing a great conflict, the danger factor becomes really high after the first 45 minutes. From 50—55 minutes the danger factor is grossly high. From 55 minutes onwards, so much energy was taken from the structure of the medium that only an Adept could possibly survive this type of legitimate deep trance condition. This, coupled with the fact that, during all of these actions, the thought impulses radiating from The Master Aetherius as He described these actions, were picked up and translated by the mind of the medium. In some parts of these actions, these thought impulses were passing through the brain, nervous system and larynx of the medium at stupendous velocities — so quickly in fact that even though Doctor King was in the enhanced condition of the much-sought-after Samadhi, it took tremendous physical and mental energy to bring about the translation of these very high velocity thought impulses into sound — the English language. This should give you a better appreciation of what 24 such Transmissions meant to the physical structure of the author, the average length of which was 60 minutes, 31 seconds.

It is a miracle that he lived through this painful and exacting ordeal and could not have survived without true, deep faith in God which he continually demonstrated.

And thus ended the titanic struggle, with life and freedom of the masses as the prize.

There were times of triumph during "Operation Karmalight."

There were times of suffering during "Operation Karmalight."

But one of the saddest facts of all, connected with this Mission, was the fact that Six Beings fought and suffered on your behalf without the vast majority of the world knowing anything about it.

That The Adepts manipulated Karma on behalf of every living entity on Earth during "Operation Karmalight" is one of the great Truths of your history. There will come a time when Karma must be balanced. That time will demand some type of repayment to be made by every sentient being on Earth to The Adepts for what They did for all men. This is not only the opinion of the author, but is based on the statements of the Ancient Cosmic Masters, Who have deep knowledge and appreciation of the all-pervasive, unchanging Law of Karma.

If the successful conclusion of "Operation Karmalight" and the defeat and transmutation of satan had been the only Mission which The Six Adepts had performed for you, They still would stand as the most helpful Beings in your history, but this was not all as you have already read in this book. (Note 1.)

A SYNOPSIS OF OPERATION KARMALIGHT

PHASE			DATE
No. 1	—	"The War Clouds"	October 26th, 1967.
No. 2	—	"Attack"	November 8th, 1967.
No. 3	—	"Ghost Ship"	November 29th, 1967.
No. 4	—	"Sabotage"	December 9th, 1967.
No. 5	—	"Commando Tactics"	January 10th, 1968.
No. 6	—	"The Worm Bites"	February 2nd/3rd, 1968.
No. 7	—	"The Assassin"	March 11th, 1968.
No. 8	—	(Silent)	April 2nd, 1968.
No. 9	—	(Silent)	April 15th, 1968.
No. 10	—	(Silent)	April 23rd, 1968.
No. 11	—	"The New Weapon"	May 14th, 1968.
No. 12	—	"Backfire"	May 29th, 1968.
No. 13	—	"The V.I.P."	June 12th, 1968.
No. 14	—	"The Masquerade"	June 21st, 1968.
No. 15	—	"Put The Home Fires Out"	July 8th, 1968.
No. 16	—	"Exploration"	August 2nd, 1968.
No. 17	—	"Emergency"	August 9th, 1968.
No. 18	—	"The Great White Brotherhood Is Taught A Lesson"	September 2nd, 1968.

No. 19 —	*"It Takes Six Good Men To Pull Three Deadly Teeth"*	October 17th, 1968.
No. 20 —	*"The Probe"*	November 6th, 1968.
No. 21 —	*"The She Devil"*	December 2nd, 1968.
No. 22 —	*"Plot And Counterplot"*	December 5th, 1968.
No. 23 —	*"The Temple Of Sacrifice"*	January 16th, 1969.
No. 24 —	*"To Catch A Devil"*	February 24th, 1969.

AUTHOR'S RECOMMENDATIONS

Note 1.

A brief but very enlightening account of "Operation Karmalight" as the Mission was proceeding was reported in The Aetherius Society Newsletter. These reports are contained in Newsletters, Volume 6, Issue 22, November 1967 through Volume 7, Issue 24, November 1968; and Volume 8, Issues 1 & 2, January 1969 through Issues 8—10, April/May 1969.

Readers are also recommended to study cassette no. C-55, *"The Men Who Won Operation Karmalight For You,"* for a deep insight into the tremendous difficulties and limitations under which The Adepts operated.

CHAPTER FIVE

FURTHER ACTION BY THE SIX ADEPTS

Not content to bask in the glories of the successful conclusion of "Operation Karmalight" and the other actions already described in this book, The Six Adepts forged ahead to further protect life on this Planet as mankind was not sufficiently advanced to protect himself. It is true to say that never before since mankind has been on the Planet Earth have six Beings done so much for him. The Cosmic Masters have made this statement very clear to all of us and when we examine the lists of massive accomplishments of The Adepts, we must agree.

AFTERMATH OF OPERATION KARMALIGHT

As soon as it became known in the hells that the supreme dictator had been transmuted, a political, magical and military power conflict gradually became evident. Without going into too long an explanation, this power conflict was roughly divided into two major camps — the military and the priesthood. According to Karmic Law and to preserve what may be termed as "general peace" on the lower astral Realms, it was necessary for The Adepts to start another Mission which was called, "The Aftermath Of Operation Karmalight." At the time of the revision of this book, "The Aftermath Of Operation Karmalight," is still proceeding and may continue, as far as we know, into the future. However, The Adepts, up to this time, have performed eleven Phases of this Mission, very carefully done in accordance with the strict Laws of Karma, to not only preserve some semblance of peace on the lower Realms, but also to educate, teach and uplift the entities who reside there. (Note 1.)

A SYNOPSIS OF THE AFTERMATH OF OPERATION KARMALIGHT

PHASE		DATE
No. 1.	*"Lubek & Egog"*	May 28th, 1969.
No. 2.	*"Plans Of Lubek"*	June 1st, 1969.
No. 3.	*"Block 5 Versus The New Laser"*	October 14th, 1969.
No. 4.	*"The Liberators"*	June 14th, 1970.
No. 5.	*"Drug Master"*	June 16th, 1970.
No. 6.	*"The Council Of 13"*	July 11th, 1970.
No. 7.	*"The Meeting Of The 500"*	July 24th, 1970.
No. 8.	*"The Assassins"*	January 20th, 1971.
No. 9.	*"The Door Opens"*	September 30th, 1975.
No. 10.	*"Overthrow Of The Covens Of Koll"*	October 1st, 1975.
No. 11.	*"The Elaborate Traps"*	October 11th, 1975.

There were three more secret sorties during 1979.
The Adepts continue to remain on standby.

WORLD EMERGENCY

Expulsion of alien Spacecraft from Level Five of Earth. (Note 2.)

5 Distinct Phases, Between October 22nd, 1972 and November 24th, 1972.

THE ATOMIC MISSION

A dangerous mutated radioactive life-form in the lower astral Realms had grown out of control. The Five Adepts contained and destroyed this menace. (Note 3.)

9 Distinct Phases, Between December 5th, 1972 and February 14th, 1973.

THE AFTERMATH OF THE ALIEN MISSION

The Five Adepts, acting directly upon instructions from The Spiritual Hierarchy Of The Solar System — The Lords Of Saturn — without hesitation, started another dangerous Mission in the lower astral Realms on December 2nd, 1974. In this Mission, The Adepts went after five Spacecraft designed by the alien before it was expelled from the lower Realms on October 26th, 1965. These craft were heavily armed with very dangerous weaponry, far in advance of other weapons on Earth. The biggest fear was not so much the weaponry being used by denizens from the lower astral Realms as the fact that, under certain conditions, the generators supplying the motive power to these craft and to the weapons aboard, could be run into seizure causing an explosion far worse than many hydrogen bombs. These craft had to be found and destroyed before this could happen.

As soon as the orders were issued by one of The Lords Of The Inner Hierarchal Council upon Saturn, Adepts Zero Zero Five, Zero Zero Four and Zero Zero Two took Their own Spacecraft to Satellite No. 3 in order to have some modifications done on it. This made the search and intercepter craft more powerful and more capable of handling the difficult and dangerous assignment.

SYNOPSIS OF THE AFTERMATH OF THE ALIEN MISSION

PHASE		DATE
No. 1.	*"Capture Of Alien Spacecraft"*	December 2, 1974.
No. 2.	*"Perhaps Two For The Price Of One"*	December 5, 1974.
No. 3.	*"We Will Have To Fight For This One"*	December 9, 1974.
No. 4.	(Silent)	December 1974.
No. 5.	*"An Oscar May Be Deserved"*	December 12, 1974.

OTHER SORTIES IN THE LOWER ASTRAL REALMS

"Samurai Contract"   March 5, 1973
Special Mission performed with   October 21, 1973.
Karmic Permission.

SPECIAL POWER TRANSMISSIONS

Special Power Transmission "Standard Type" 1
Special Emergency, December 1967 1
Power Transmission Using Basic Cooperators in Blocks 1
Operation One One One (after July 8th, 1964) 1

                         Total 4

                                            (Note 4.)

SPECIAL STAND-BY PERIODS

    The Ascended Masters on Shamballa, under the leadership of The Lord Buddha, and The Spiritual Hierarchy Of Earth, under the leadership of The Lord Babaji, together hold the Light on behalf of all life streams on Earth. So precarious is the overall Karmic pattern of the masses that any substantial movement from either Shamballa or The Spiritual Hierarchy must be compensated for. If, for instance, it becomes necessary for Ascended Masters from The Spiritual Hierarchy to leave Their physical Retreats on Earth to travel even to Shamballa for Initiations, then while They are away, it is essential that Psychic Centres and danger spots on Earth be manned by other Entities. For instance, if there is a movement from the physical Retreats of Earth to another part of the Solar System for even a short time, this weakens the manpower, for that time, of The Spiritual Hierarchy. In order to make up for this, a simple but brilliantly effective procedure is adopted. This always involves The Adepts and other chosen people living on Earth who are sent to specific areas of great danger. His Eminence, Sir George King has been asked to cooperate in these Stand-Bys and has been ordered to certain places during a movement of Ascended Masters from Their physical Retreats on Earth. As a further illustration, the overall Manipulators of the Stand-By Periods know that while Sir

George King is on the Psychic Centre in Utah, beneath Padre Bay, Lake Powell, that no catastrophe of a serious nature can occur because such a catastrophe would also kill him. Therefore, he is moved into that position for the length of the Stand-By Period. It is the same with The Six Adepts Who are always involved during these Stand-By Periods in one way or another. Sometimes if The Lord Babaji Himself has to leave Earth for Initiatory or other reasons, then His place is always taken by another Master from The Spiritual Hierarchy or even by a Master from another Planet as a temporary measure. This type of Mission is a recurring one and, as far as the author is concerned, not only a great honour to him, but, for the most part, an extremely pleasant, uplifting experience. (Note 5.)

To the time of publication there have been ten Stand-By Periods.

OPERATION SUNBEAM

Twenty-one Special Phases were performed by The Spiritual Hierarchy of Earth in cooperation with The Six Adepts and the Masters from the Star System "Gotha."

This Mission started on September 28th, 1976, and ended on October 17th, 1976, during which time tremendous energies were given directly to The Logos Of Earth in deference for what The Aetherius Society had already done in "Operation Sunbeam," and as a partial repayment for mankind's colossal debt to The Goddess, Terra.

Later, The Adepts agreed to help The Spiritual Hierarchy Of Earth build the necessary apparatus for a full-scale extension of "Operation Sunbeam" on December 5th, 1978. (Note 6.)

OPERATION SPACE MAGIC

The next step taken by The Six Adepts to potentize "Operation Sunbeam" even further took the form of a new Mission called, "Operation Space Magic."

This Mission extended "Operation Sunbeam" onto an Interplanetary basis by allowing Spiritual Energies to be collected from other Planets in this Solar System and manipulated into Psychic Centres within the Body of the Planet Earth.

When you consider that leading astrologers are predicting more and more world catastrophe as we go further into the "Jupiter Effect" period of 1980-1984, the brilliant strategy and timing of this Mission become even more apparent.

The astrological pressures which are building up during the period of 1980-1984 are predicted to bring about more and more wars, earthquakes, droughts and floods. However, if highly elevated Spiritual Energies are passed from certain of the Planets to the Earth during this time, then this has the effect of relieving some of these undesirable astrological pressures and preventing much of the destruction and suffering which would have been our fate were it not for The Six Adepts.

During the period March 5th-9th, 1980, The Six Adepts placed specialized modules upon the Planets Saturn, Jupiter, Venus and Neptune. On January 23rd, 1981, They placed a Satellite in orbit of this Earth which has an operating and orbital expectancy of over 1,000 years. This Satellite was designed to receive high frequencies of Spiritual Energies from the modules on Saturn, Jupiter, Venus and Neptune in order that they can be readily collected by the Masters from Gotha during Phases of "Operation Sunbeam."

So important is this Interplanetary manipulation of Spiritual Energy at this time that arrangements were made to start Phases of "Operation Sunbeam" of this kind on July 28th, 1980. On this date two Phases were performed by the Masters from Gotha which resulted in Spiritual Energies being collected from Venus and Jupiter and transmitted into the Psychic Centre in Scotland. (Note 7.)

OPERATION PRAYER POWER

THE ADEPTS ASSISTED IN THE MANIPULATION OF SPIRITUAL ENERGY DURING THESE OPERATION PRAYER POWER DISCHARGES

PHASE — DURATION — DATE — DESTINATION

No. 1   August 20th, 1973   To those working to help the flood
        3 hrs.   victims in Northwest India and West Pakistan.

No. 2	December 15/16, 1973 2hrs., 42mins.	To Northern India where a severe cholera epidemic had been predicted. The epidemic did not develop.
No. 3	July 21/22, 1974 3hrs., 20mins.	To peacemakers gathered in the United Nations in New York and in Cyprus, to avert an all-out war between Greece and Turkey. Within hours a first ceasefire was called.
No. 4	August 26, 1974 3hrs., 34mins.	Again war threatened between Greece and Turkey. A second discharge was sent to the peacemakers and within a few days, new ceasefire arrangements were agreed upon.
No. 5	September 24, 1974 1hr., 47mins.	To agencies working for the relief of the victims of Hurricane "Fifi" which swept Honduras, the Islas de Bahia and Belieze on September 18, 1974.
No. 7	June 22, 1977 39 mins. July 5, 1977 22mins.	Energy released to help overcome bad interference during the performance of "Operation Sunbeam" in the British Isles.
Cambodia	November 13, 1979 2hrs., 52mins.	To aid those helping the starving refugees in Cambodia.
Iran	November 26, 1979	The Adepts invoked 560 Prayer Hours of A+ energy and directed this to Iran for peace.
Iraq/Iran	2hrs., 38mins. September 27/28, 1980	The Adepts manipulated 633 Prayer Hours of energy from The Aetherius Society plus 1,179 Prayer Hours from The Great White Brotherhood in an attempt to bring a peaceful settlement in the war between Iran and Iraq.

Algeria	October 11, 1980 2hrs., 46mins.	1,063 Prayer Hours of energy, plus 1,078 Prayer Hours of A+ energy from The Great White Brotherhood, were manipulated by The Adepts to bring relief to the earthquake victims in Algiers. During this time they also directed 845 Prayer Hours from The Great White Brotherhood to Iran and Iraq.
Italy	November 24, 1980 2hrs., 15mins.	Following a severe earthquake in Italy, The Adepts manipulated 440 Prayer Hours of energy from The Aetherius Society, plus 3,885 Prayer Hours from The Great White Brotherhood, to bring relief to the thousands of victims in that area. (Note 8.)

January 1st, 1978.

The Master Aetherius announced in His Transmission, *"Important Declaration Of Truth To Terra,"* that The Six Adepts and The Great White Brotherhood would search the Realms to locate trusted agencies for the extension of "Operation Prayer Power" to those Realms. (Note 9.)

September 23rd, 1979.

With the help of The Adepts, "Operation Prayer Power" was Inaugurated on Level Four of Earth. (Note 10.)

November 26th, 1979.

A Battery was Charged with 1,250 Prayer Hours of A+ energy by The Adepts with Spiritual Energy from 19 Holy Mountains and additional valuable information concerning specific properties of these Mountains were given. (Note 11.)

OTHER OPERATIONS

April 28th, 1968.

Adepts Zero Zero Four and Zero Zero Five transported Batteries from The Great White Brotherhood Retreats to the new Satellite called, The Shamballa Annex and installed computers thereon.

December 18th, 1975.

The Adepts participated in the rescue of the occupants of an alien Spacecraft which crashed on Level Two.

December 3rd, 1978.

An animal rescue clinic was formed on the Spirit Realms by Adepts Zero Zero Four and Zero Zero Five to specifically deal with the auras of animals which had met a sudden and violent death on Earth.

AUTHOR'S RECOMMENDATIONS

No. 1.

For a report on the First two Phases of "The Aftermath Of Operation Karmalight," study The Aetherius Society Newsletter, Volume 8, Issues 13-15, July/August, 1969.

No. 2.

Towards the end of 1972, life on Earth was threatened by the arrival of alien intelligences who, while not belligerent, nevertheless embarked on a mission very dangerous to all Levels of life on this Planet. A report of this emergency and the action taken by The Adepts to protect mankind can be read in The Aetherius Society Newsletter, Volume 11, Issue 14, October 1972, and Volume 12, Issues 1-3, January/February 1973.

Note 3.

For a study of this dangerous and very hazardous Mission, read the booklet, *"The Atomic Mission."*

Note 4.

For further information on these Special Power Transmissions, read The Aetherius Society Newsletters, Volume 7, Issues 1 & 2, January 1968; Issue 21, October 1968; Volume 10, Issues 9-12, May/June 1971; Volume 12, Issues 21 & 22, October 1973.

Note 5.

Full reports of some of these Stand-By Periods have been published by The Aetherius Society, and readers are recommended to study the following for a greater understanding of these important occasions: Newsletter, Volume 14, Issues 21-24, December 1975; the booklet, *"A Special Assignment";* and a unique cassette album containing the author's on-the-spot report of a Stand-By, together with a lecture and two Cosmic Transmissions, Metacassette® no. MC-10, *"Watcher In The Night."*

Note 6.

"Operation Sunbeam" is a Cosmic Mission, designed by His Eminence, Sir George King and performed by The Aetherius Society, in which Spiritual Energies, originally intended for the use of mankind, are directed through specialized equipment into certain Psychic Centres of Earth as a token repayment for the vast energy debt owed by mankind to The Logos Of Earth. The vast Karmic implications of this Mission have made it, according to Cosmic Sources, **the single most important task being undertaken on Earth by any organization or even country** and an integral part of the Cosmic Plan for world Salvation and Enlightenment. By Karmic Law certain outside assistance has been allowed and Three Masters from an advanced Solar System, known as Gotha, are resident upon Earth to help the Mission which has been immensely potentized by Their intervention. This assistance is the direct result of help rendered to the Gotha System by The Adepts. Readers are recommended to listen to Metacassette® no. MC-19, *"Gotha Speaks To Earth."* Further intervention by Higher Forces was allowed in "Operation Sunbeam" in 1976 and a full report of the 21 Special Phases can be read in The Aetherius Society Newsletter, Volume 15, Issues 20-22, November 1976.

Amazing Revelations on the Karmic repercussions of "Operation Sunbeam," together with a report on the meeting of The Spiritual Hierarchy Of Earth at which the author's permission was given to The Spiritual Hierarchy to perform this Mission, are contained in the booklet, *"Operation Sunbeam—God's Magic In Action."*

Readers are also recommended to study the following: Cassette no. C-54, *"Operation Sunbeam,"* Metacassette® MC-2, *"Operation Sunbeam Inspires The Galaxy!"* and The Aetherius Society Newsletters: Volume 5, Issues 10-12, May/June 1966; Issues 13 & 14, July 1966; Volume 6, Issues 1-5, January/February 1967; Volume 11, Issues 9 &10, July 1972; Issues 19-24, December 1972; Volume 15, Issues 13-16, August/September 1976; Volume 16, Issue 22, October 1977; Volume 18, Issues 19-22, October 1979; Issues 29-32, November/December 1979; Volume 19, Issues 11-14, June/July 1980.

Note 7.

For further information on "Operation Space Magic," read the book *"Operation Space Magic—The Cosmic Connection."* Details of this Mission were first published in Cosmic Voice, Volume 1, Issues 1-4, August/September 1980, and in Volume 2, Issue 1, January 1981.

Note 8.

"Operation Prayer Power," a Spiritual Mission designed by His Eminence, Sir George King, is the most potent mass Healing tool ever devised for the use and benefit of ordinary terrestrials, and was accepted into the Cosmic Plan for the Salvation and Enlightenment of mankind on September 2nd, 1975. In this Mission, Prayer Energy invoked by dedicated people is stored in specially designed Spiritual Energy Batteries which can be released at any time to any part of the world where disaster strikes. For further information on this vitally important Mission, study of the following material is recommended: Cassette no. C-52, *"Operation Prayer Power;"* Metacassette® no. MC-12, *"Operation Prayer Power—A Spiritual Dream Come True;"* The Aetherius Society Newsletters: Volume 11, Issue 5, March 1972; Volume 12, Issues 14-17, August 1973; Volume 17, Issues 5-8, March/April 1978; Issue 19, August 1978; Volume 18, Issues 23-26, October 1979; Issues 33 & 34, December 1979; Cosmic Voice, Volume 1, Issues 5-8, October/November 1980.

Further details on Phases 1 through 7 referred to are contained in Newsletters: Volume 12, Issues 26 &27, December 1973; Volume 13, Issues 16-20, August/September 1974; Issues 25 & 26, December 1974; Volume 14, Issue 18, September 1975; Volume 15, Issues 5 & 6, March 1976; Volume 16, Issues 23-25, November 1977.

Note 9.

Details of the tremendous significance of "Operation Prayer Power" to the Spiritual progress of mankind were revealed in a vitally important Transmission from The Master Aetherius and, together with a detailed explanation by the author, is available on Metacassette® no. MC-13, *"Important Declaration Of Truth To Terra."*

Note 10.

Listen to Metacassette® no. MC-21, *"The Inauguration Of Operation Prayer Power On Level Four,"* for a brilliant description of this majestic event at which the author, as the designer of the Mission, initiated the charging of the first Spiritual Energy Battery on the Higher Realms.

Note 11.

Nineteen Mountains throughout the world were charged with Spiritual Energy by the Cosmic Masters between July 23rd, 1958 and August 23rd, 1961, during an immensely important Metaphysical Operation called, "Operation Starlight." His Eminence, Sir George King was used as a channel for the initial charge to be put into 18 of these Mountains. The Holy Mountains charged during "Operation Starlight" are now gigantic batteries of Spiritual Energy which any ordinary person can contact through Prayer and radiate to the world as a whole. They also provide the Spiritual Energy source which is radiated to The Logos Of Earth during "Operation Sunbeam."

For further details on this Mission, read the booklet, *"Holy Mountains Of The World,"* and listen to cassette no. C-27, *"Deep Occult Revelations About Operation Starlight."*

Note 12.

Read The Aetherius Society Newsletter, Volume 18, Issues 5-8, April/May 1979.